JUL - - 2021

MIDLOTHIAN PUBLIC LIBRARY
W9-AXA-778

A Guide to Writing College Admissions Essays

A Guide to Writing College Admissions Essays

Practical Advice for Students and Parents

Cory M. Franklin, Suzanne Franklin,
Linda Black, Paul Weingarten

ROWMAN & LITTLEFIELD
Lanham • Boulder • New York • London

Published by Rowman & Littlefield
An imprint of The Rowman & Littlefield Publishing Group, Inc.
4501 Forbes Boulevard, Suite 200, Lanham, Maryland 20706
www.rowman.com

6 Tinworth Street, London SE11 5AL, United Kingdom

British Library Cataloguing in Publication Information Available

Library of Congress Cataloging-in-Publication Data

Names: Franklin, Cory M., author.
Title: A guide to writing college admissions essays : practical advice for students and parents / Cory M. Franklin, Suzanne Franklin, Linda Black, Paul Weingarten.
Description: Lanham : Rowman & Littlefield, [2021] | Includes bibliographical references and index. | Summary: "This book is a handy, readable manual, which deals with the practical problems students face when writing their college admission essays"—Provided by publisher.
Identifiers: LCCN 2021005837 (print) | LCCN 2021005838 (ebook) | ISBN 9781475858761 (cloth) | ISBN 9781475858785 (epub)
Subjects: LCSH: College applications—Handbooks, manuals, etc. | Universities and colleges—Admission. | Exposition (Rhetoric)
Classification: LCC LB2351.5 .F73 2021 (print) | LCC LB2351.5 (ebook) | DDC 378.1/616—dc23
LC record available at https://lccn.loc.gov/2021005837

∞™ The paper used in this publication meets the minimum requirements of American National Standard for Information Sciences—Permanence of Paper for Printed Library Materials, ANSI/NISO Z39.48-1992.

Four authors mean more dedications to people we love.

From Cory and Sue: *For Shana, Celia, Jeff, Sam, Neta, and Charlotte*
And for James and Sabina Jean

From Linda: *For Rich, Maddie, Carlie, and my mom Aggie*

From Paul: *To Marla and Elizabeth, who never cease to inspire me*

Vigorous writing is concise. A sentence should contain no unnecessary words, a paragraph no unnecessary sentences, for the same reason a drawing should have no unnecessary lines and a machine no unnecessary parts. This requires not that the writer make all his sentences short or that he avoid all detail and treat his subject only in outline, but that every word tell.

—Professor William Strunk, lead author of *Elements of Style*

Contents

Preface

Share an essay on any topic of your choice. It can be one you've already written, one that responds to a different prompt, or one of your own design.

Discuss an accomplishment, event, or realization that sparked a period of personal growth and a new understanding of yourself or others.

The lessons we take from obstacles we encounter can be fundamental to later success. Recount a time when you faced a challenge, setback, or failure. How did it affect you, and what did you learn from the experience?

Every year thousands of panicky high school students confront these questions and others like them, hoping to impress college admissions officers who are harder than ever to impress. Students and parents know the stakes are high. A teen's college admission may be riding on this essay. No wonder students often approach the college essay with dread: What to write? How to present yourself without looking like you're trying too hard or stretching credulity?

These students seek help from parents, teachers, peers, siblings, and private tutors to improve their essays—and their odds of acceptance. Many students succeed because they craft memorable essays that stand out as funny or insightful or poignant.

But thousands of others grind out works that fall flat. Reasons? That's easy. Lifeless prose that reveals little of a student's personality. Threadbare or hackneyed themes that admissions officers have seen a zillion times before. Writing riddled with misspellings and grammatical errors.

Avalanched under increasing numbers of applications, colleges look for quick ways to sort the "Acceptances" from the "Waiting Lists" from the "Rejections."

That is why you are reading this book.

First a disclaimer: College admissions officers work in mysterious ways; test scores, legacies, and demographics all play a role in whether a student is admitted. Today, some universities and colleges receive more than fifty thousand applications for a limited number of positions. This guide to better writing doesn't guarantee a spot at Stanford or Vanderbilt. Nothing can do that. A great essay is usually not enough by itself. But the college essay is a vital part of that process, even though admission committees are notoriously reticent about what they are specifically looking for in an essay or exactly how crucial the essay is to the application. This varies from school to school. The essay is certainly more important at some schools like the University of Chicago, which emphasizes its own "out of the box" essay questions—for example, "compare Plato and Play-Doh" or "Find x." In addition, as greater numbers of schools adopt "test-optional" or "test-blind" policies, which minimize or eliminate the need to take the SAT or the ACT, the college essay will definitely assume greater significance.

In this book you'll find suggestions on what to write (and just as important, what *not* to write) and vital tips on writing approach, grammar, and usage. This guide isn't just for college-bound students. It's for anyone at any age who wants to write better, clearer, crisper.

This book is a team effort. Two of its authors are college counselors with more than twenty years of experience helping students gain acceptance to their first choice of college. In the process, they have read thousands of college essays. And they have the psychic scars to prove it. The other two authors are writers, one a former senior editor, writer, and member of the *Chicago Tribune* Editorial Board and the other an intensive care physician turned essayist with four books to his credit. They have used their collective experience to create a manual that will help students write excellent college essays.

This book is meant as a guide for students facing the 650-word Common App essay and the supplementary essays that many schools require as part of their admission applications. With more students applying to college and those students applying to an ever-increasing number of schools, the college admission process is far more competitive than ever before.

If there is one point of unanimity about the college admission essay it is this: that it must be authentic—a true reflection of the writer's character and personality. Colleges take great pains to learn who you are and one way, perhaps the most important way outside of a live interview, is the essay. The essay's content and style reveal much about who the writer is—in some cases, even more than the live interview.

There are excellent reference websites such as *Grammarly*, style guides such as *Elements of Style* and *The Chicago Manual of Style*, and videos for writers. Most skilled writers know when to use these references. The authors of this book recommend their use. This book is meant to complement rather than replace them because most high school students lack the experience to know when and how to use those aids effectively. The value of this book is its additional advice to the writer about content and style.

The target audience for this book is those students and the people who help them with their essays: parents, English teachers, and writing centers (none of whom should help *too* much). It is for students without an extensive writing background who must write concise and clear essays. Because it is written with a specific goal in mind—the college essay—readers will find information that might be hard to locate in a general style guide. This convenience should be attractive to students who will be busy with school, extracurriculars, and preparing the other aspects of their college applications.

This book is a handy manual that deals with the practical problems faced when writing the college essay, one that users can keep on their desks, take with them, or refer to in a writing center. We hope you can find tips you can use, not just for essays but in college and beyond. Our goal is to help you craft a readable, compelling essay that will engage the reader and give you a creative voice along with the means to express yourself. It just might make a difference in the final admission process.

Acknowledgments

We wish to thank all the students we have worked with over the years. They are the ones who were the inspiration for this book, as well as being responsible for its creation. We especially want to thank the students who gave us permission to use their college essays. Their well-crafted essays not only made the book possible, they made it better as well. (We tried to avoid the overused "not only *x* but also *y*" construction by omitting the "but." Some grammarians may not agree.) We have no doubt some of these students will go on to be splendid writers.

For his longtime (not "long time") support and counsel over the years, we are grateful to Mr. Jim Conroy. Mr. Conroy, which is how he is known to his students (in the manner of Mr. Chips), was a college counselor at New Trier High School in Winnetka, Illinois, for forty years and was generally acknowledged to be the best in the business. We thought so highly of his advice that we included an interview with him in this book. We urge you to read that interview and give regard to his wise words.

Sid Tepps and Betsy Collins each played a vital role in the preparation of this book. Sid was always available when we had a computer problem—and we had many of them. There was no problem he couldn't solve. Betsy introduced us to the wonderful people at Rowman & Littlefield, who believed in us when we approached them with our proposal.

Finally, thanks to the people at Rowman & Littlefield—Carlie Wall, Tom Koerner, and Jed Lyons. Their help at every step of the way was invaluable, especially because the book was written at the height of the COVID-19 crisis. We hope that we have repaid their faith in us with this book.

Introduction

This is a message to all high school students preparing to write a Common App essay: Don't panic. You *can* do this. And this book can help.

You probably will not have time to read this book cover to cover, but you can still benefit from it. Select a chapter or a couple of pages to guide you through each step of writing your essay: picking the best essay prompt, brainstorming what to write, actually writing the essay, editing what you have written, and creating the final draft that leads to that satisfying moment when you hit "Submit."

Right now, that seems a long way off. You've got a blank computer screen. And maybe a mind to match. But don't worry. It's understandable if you dread this assignment. Writing the Common App essay is one of the more formidable tasks a writer can take on. In most writing, authors aim to communicate with certain readers; the writer knows the intended audience. A college admission essay, however, has a limited audience—the admissions officers who will read your application. What do you, as a high school student, know about these anonymous but all-powerful readers? Little to nothing. Moreover, the pressure is on—a college admission essay matters more than most other types of writing you've done.

If you're a typical high school student, you don't have a lot of essay writing experience and aren't accustomed to a strict deadline and a hard 650-word count. (If you are one of those students who chafes at the 650-word count of the Common App essay, be warned: The Common App software cuts off all essays at that point, no exceptions.)

No wonder you are fearful; even seasoned writers would be intimidated by all this.

The good news is that you have more help than most writers do. Besides websites, style guides, and this book, you have your parents, teachers, writing centers, and college counselors. Use them—but don't rely on them too much. They can certainly help, but ultimately the essay must come from you. And it must be genuine: your inspiration, your voice. We advise all our students that no matter what subject they write about or how they write it, the essay must be *heartfelt and honest*. Those are the two guiding qualities we look for in every essay, and they are the same qualities college admissions readers look for. Experienced college admissions readers are hard to fool. They have read thousands of essays, and they are experts at spotting insincerity and phoniness. Remember—a good essay may not guarantee you admission, but a bad one will almost certainly guarantee rejection.

You will probably hear that your admission essay provides colleges with an idea of who you are, but there is something even more important about the essay. It provides you with an opportunity for introspection—a chance to glimpse inside yourself. It demands you draw on your experience, creativity, and imagination. This is how you hone your narrative abilities.

In many respects, a successful Common App essay is not defined solely by whether it helps you gain admission to your top choice. It also helps you to understand yourself better—just as any good piece of writing, fiction or nonfiction, does for a writer.

There is no one correct way, no formula, to write a strong Common App essay. This means you can be creative. You can use humor, write dialogue, or craft a descriptive essay with an emphasis on point of view, sights, and sounds. These essays can be particularly effective if they are done well. Be aware, however, that these creative conventions are difficult to master, even for experienced writers. There is a fine line between being creative and relying on gimmicks. The student who is overly concerned with trying to be creative at the expense of trying to be sincere often winds up with an unreadable essay. There are few things worse than a humor essay that is not funny or dialogue that comes off as stilted.

The one thing you don't want is for a college essay reader to toss your piece aside after a few sentences. With thousands of essays to go through in a limited number of weeks, admission readers go through submissions quickly, and it is probably impossible for them to read every essay thoroughly. In fact, some schools are employing artificial intelligence using algorithms with proprietary characteristics to screen essays. (What are these algorithms looking for? Clichés? Certain buzz words or phrases? We don't know.)

In that respect, here are some general guidelines that we will elaborate on throughout the book. Answer the essay prompt you have selected and try to grab the reader's attention with a strong opening. Show, don't tell, the reader why your subject matters. Edit yourself mercilessly. Cut extraneous words. Your essay should be lean and muscular; make every word count. Emphasize important details, but stay away from clichés. Pick the details you include carefully. Your closing paragraph is as important as your opening. In some way, try to circle back to your opening in your conclusion. When you are finished, read the essay over to yourself and then read it over out loud. Have someone you trust read it as well and consider what he or she says, but don't make changes reflexively. Edit, and then edit again. (Don't be obsessed with the 650-word count on your first draft. If it is longer, just write your story, then edit it to 650 words or less.)

Much of this is harder than it sounds. It takes motivation, effort, and time (and you don't always have a lot of time). But if you are successful, you can turn out an essay that will capture the reader. One of our students used his successful Common App essay as his valedictory speech at his high school graduation. He received a standing ovation from his classmates, something he never imagined when he set out to write his essay. Every essay doesn't turn out this well, but it gives you an idea of what is possible.

Don't worry. We're here to help you. It's going to turn out all right. Now the hardest part: Let's get started.

Chapter One

Starting Out: Confronting the Blank Screen

The Pulitzer Prize–winning sportswriter Red Smith described how difficult beginning a writing assignment can be, "Writing is easy. You just open a vein and bleed." There isn't a writer alive who, at one time or another, hasn't struggled at the start, confronting the fearsome blank screen or, in the days before computers, the blank page.

And here you are, facing pressures of all sorts—school, social, home, finishing college applications, job, and whatever else is going on in your life—and you must compose a Common App essay. You may still be experiencing writer's block even if you have already selected your prompt. Maybe you still haven't figured out what to write about; maybe you're just afraid or worried that your essay won't be good enough.

There is only one solution to writer's block—start writing. Anything. *It's your first draft and not your final essay.* Sounds easy, but it's not. So what do you do?

Brainstorm. Do not underestimate the importance of brainstorming when you start out; it can be useful in preventing the dilemma of a blank screen. Consider brainstorming with your parents or whoever has helped you with your resume. That can be a good springboard for possible essay topics: your feelings about something personal, whether it is a memorable event, person, or experience. Remember that your focus must be using the topic you choose to tell the reader about yourself.

Control your writing environment. Everything: time, place, and atmosphere. Make yourself as comfortable as possible. To begin, carve out at least half an hour of time that will not interfere with your schoolwork.

(As your college counselors will tell you, it is exceedingly important to keep your grades up during the first quarter or semester of your senior year because colleges request those grades and pay attention to them. So don't sacrifice critical study time for your essay.) Your essay may take anywhere from a week to a month, sometimes longer, so begin early. You have a specific deadline, no excuses. Find a place where you are comfortable writing, one with as few distractions as possible. *This means a space with no television or video games. Turn off the cell phone.* When you are writing you absolutely cannot multitask. If you are someone who can write with soft music in the background, go ahead and listen. But once the music becomes a distraction, turn it off. Writing demands full concentration. Then, just commit something to the screen.

You don't have to start at the beginning. If you can't find an opening, start in the middle. Or somewhere else. The point: Don't get hung up.

Some students freeze because they think they must write in a set order: a beginning, middle, and end. If you have a good hook to reel in the reader, great. You can begin with that as an opening paragraph and work from there. But the good hook, although desirable, is not crucial. Many students don't have that hook when they begin.

You may have a general idea about what you're going to write about, maybe your summer job or your family or the problem you want to solve. On the first draft, write whatever comes to your mind—even if it is just key words and not even complete sentences. Making a brief outline of your points helps. Save what you have written. These thoughts may immediately prompt you to write complete sentences or even a paragraph or two. Go ahead, keep going if you can. Alternatively, you may simply put those words or sentences away, so it gives you something to think about the next time you sit down to write your essay. Either way, set a goal for your first writing session—if not a certain number of words, then a good idea of where you are going with the essay.

More likely than not, when you fill these thoughts in, they will become part of the body of your essay. Your opening and your concluding paragraph will come later. The point is that quite often the way to overcome writer's block is to start by writing ideas and then elaborate later as you go, not by starting at the beginning and working from there. If you are still stuck after writing a couple of words or sentences, read what you do have to someone you trust, especially if he or she has something to do with your story (e.g., your best friend, boyfriend or girlfriend, parent); they may help you begin filling in the blanks.

To illustrate how a good essay can come from just your thoughts and notes, consider this anecdote from Tom Wolfe, widely acknowledged as one of the top writers in the United States during the last generation. Wolfe often told a story about how he overcame writer's block on his first *New York Magazine* assignment. When he couldn't produce the story, his frustrated editors finally told him to send his notes, "and we'll give them to a real writer—they didn't say 'real'—to put into proper form, . . . and with a very heavy heart, I said O.K. and I sat down to write out the notes." As Wolfe told it, the editor simply removed the greeting at the top and published the "notes" as *The Kandy-Kolored Tangerine-Flake Streamline Baby*. That book became a best seller and one of the most acclaimed books of its time—all from nothing more than his notes. Your essay can come from your notes.

You have a fixed word count, but that's for your final draft. Don't obsess over that on your first draft.

Your essay must be 650 words or less when you submit, but when you are writing the first draft, aim for somewhere between 450 and 850 words. When you come back to the essay, if it is short you can add detail (although you are not obligated to use all 650 words for your final essay). If it is long, you can edit it down. Don't be paralyzed by the word count.

Once you have confronted writer's block and started to formulate your essay, essentially you have to write three separate parts: the introduction, the body, and the conclusion. The introduction and the conclusion are usually about one paragraph each, both generally between fifty and one hundred words, and we will discuss them briefly later in the chapter.

The body of the essay is where you tell your story. It is "the meat" of your essay—in effect, your personal statement. Within reason, you shouldn't worry about how long or how short it is—it should generally be around three to six hundred words. If it is on the short side, you can expand it or write a longer introduction or conclusion. If it is on the long side, you can edit after you have written your introduction and conclusion.

Remember, no matter what you are writing about, the body of the essay is about you—about what you have learned, how you have grown, an ethical problem you've faced, or what captivates you—so don't burden your essay with extraneous detail that distracts the reader. Detail can be interesting, but it can also muddy your message. That excess detail is the first thing that you will have to edit if your early draft runs long.

Once you are satisfied with the body of your essay, you can start writing the introduction and your conclusion. They are both important in illustrating more about you. Some readers, pressed for time, may only scan your introduction and your conclusion. Which should you write first? It depends. This is one of the places where there is no automatic answer, and you have to use your judgment. Remember, your essay must keep the reader engaged.

Chapter Two

The First Step: Picking a Prompt

Roughly nine hundred schools in the United States use the Common App, as do about fifty schools internationally. For the Common App essay, there are currently seven prompts, a starting point from which to launch your essay.

In December 2019, the Common App website surveyed more than ten thousand students and Common App member colleges. They found that

> the current prompts do their job well. Over 95% of every group who responded to the survey—students, counselors, teachers, admission officers—agree that the current prompts spark effective essays. That's a testament to you. Over the last 8 years, based on your feedback and the indispensable counsel of our advisory committees, we've revised and refined the prompts so they guide students toward stories that will help Common App members make informed admission decisions.

(Just a reminder that even the Common App needs an editor because numbers less than ten should be written out.)

The specific prompt you choose is not important. Some guides advise you not to start by choosing a prompt, rather to write your essay first and then select the prompt that best fits it. Our view is that students who know what they want to write should do that, but most students will need some help. You may not be sure what you will write about, and you need the assistance the prompt offers to brainstorm your essay or just to get you started. Before starting, read all the prompts, discard those you know you will not be writing about, and pick one or two of the remaining ones that look promising.

At that point, you can begin writing and gradually you will see which prompt best fits your chosen subject. You may select an identity, a setback, a challenge, a passion, or an accomplishment, and some subjects will fit more than one prompt. *No subject is better than another; it doesn't matter what you choose—much more important is how you treat your topic.*

Although your choice of prompt isn't that important, you must answer the prompt you have selected—and generally as early as possible in your essay. The most important message in your essay is telling the college reader about yourself, but the reader is also looking for several other things including how you address the task at hand and that includes your ability to follow directions. That means answering your selected prompt. No matter how beautiful your free-form essay is, you are likely to meander if you completely ignore the prompt (this is an argument for selecting a prompt before you start your essay).

It is not mandatory, but it is advisable, to answer the prompt as soon as possible in your essay, ideally in the first paragraph. Some essays don't lend themselves to answering the prompt in the first paragraph, but if you have written three hundreds words of your essay and still haven't addressed the prompt, odds are that you have probably lost the reader. (*Remember, that's the key: Don't lose the reader.*)

Answering the prompt is not simply a matter of regurgitating the prompt and then giving an answer ("The problem I would like to solve is . . ." or "I gained a new understanding of myself when . . ."). This is your chance to demonstrate your narrative ability—show, don't tell (a phrase we will come back to several times in this book). By using just a few sentences, you can explain your view of the problem you want to solve before you dive deeply into your solution. Rather than just telling the reader what your life-changing event was, briefly describe what you were like before the event occurred. These are good ways to interest the reader, answer the prompt, and transition into your narrative. In the next chapter, we will discuss these techniques in greater detail.

Don't get hung up on finding a unique idea that no one has ever written before. Your chances are not good. Most ideas have been used by countless students before you (the exception may be a problem you would like to solve). But don't let that deter you because you are convinced you must write about something special. If you do find something unique in your experience, that's great, but more important is how you tell your story. Even the most common or mundane topic—a summer job or a family vacation—can be illustrative of your personality and your voice. It can become a great essay *if you write honestly and with passion. Be authentic.*

Chapter Three

What to Do and What Not to Do When You Begin Writing

You will receive a lot of advice about what you should and shouldn't do in your essays. And there is a decent chance that some of the advice will be conflicting. Some people will tell you to add something to your essay and others will tell you to take it out. Writing your Common App essay is not an exact science, and in some cases, it's hard to determine which advice is best. Here is our take on what to do in your essay:

Build yourself up, but don't brag. No matter what you are writing about in the essay, you are telling *your* story. You want to describe your talents, your competence, the attractive aspects of your personality, and why you will be an asset to that school. This involves a modicum of self-promotion. **But remember not to reiterate the accomplishments listed in the Activities section of your Common App.** Your essay is not the place for it. If you do, the reader is likely to place it in the "Reject pile." Sometimes, you may recount something that happened to you in a competition or game, but stick to what happened and how it affected you or, as much as possible, what you learned from it instead of the outcome. If you scored the winning touchdown or hit a home run in a state championship game, talk about your emotions or the lead-up, not so much the game itself. Likewise, if you dropped the touchdown pass or struck out in the championship, you can talk about that; failure can be as compelling as success, sometimes even more so.

But here's the rub (sorry, minor cliché—see how easy it is to fall into the trap of using clichés?): There can be a fine line between self-promotion and bragging. Some admissions people say that you should brag in your essay. We do not recommend crossing that line; you can talk about yourself and still be humble, and we think humility is an important virtue to demonstrate.

It's OK to be controversial, but know your boundaries. Tread carefully with hot-button issues. You don't have to avoid "edgy" or darker topics like student suicide, but you should exercise discretion when writing about them. If you talk about sex, don't be too graphic; you risk turning off the reader. Likewise, with politics and religion; done the right way, these are both topics that can make for a good essay, as long as you remember to keep the reader interested by not becoming self-absorbed. You can talk about your political views in your essay (the school may already have an idea about your political views based on your resume), but don't make the essay about your politics or try to convince the reader of your political view. And, of course, you should always consider that the reader may not have the same political views you do—in which case, he or she just might take offense. The same with religion. Religion is an important part of many students' lives and if it is part of yours, by all means discuss it in your essay. But do not proselytize; that is another guaranteed way to ensure the reader flings your essay across the room.

If you talk about mental health issues, avoid being overly clinical and do not delve too deeply into past problems. It may be important to you, and that's fine, but the reader will want to know how you are coping rather than too much about the actual problem. Also, more students are writing about learning disabilities in their essays. We do not recommend this; a better place to explain a learning disability is in the Additional Information section of the Common App.

If you decide to write about a world problem or contemporary issue, you must put it in the context of your story. Do not make it a research paper. Issues such as climate change are popular, but in all probability your reader has read many essays about climate change and you don't want to burden the reader with details on the topic by writing a polemic. (We anticipate that the COVID-19 pandemic will also be a popular topic.) If you write about climate change or some other current problem like COVID-19, racism, homelessness, or poverty, try talking about what you are attempting to do about the problem. Perhaps you have a personal take on the issue. Readers don't want statistics or opinions, they want your story.

Don't play the "blame game." Avoid becoming a victim. Plenty of students have stories about something bad that has happened to them, something that may have been out of their control. It is tempting to write an essay portraying yourself as a victim. Resist that temptation. A "victim essay" will quickly become either maudlin or an exercise in self-absorption. Far better, if you have had something bad happen to you, that you discuss what you learned from it, how you rebounded, or how you persevered.

Profanity—it's not a good idea. Unless it's part of an important piece of dialogue—and even then, think twice—don't use profanity in your essay. It's unnecessary and can be off-putting. The same holds for controversial ethnic terms. You may know what you are trying to say, but the reader may not understand your context. If a controversial word is part of dialogue you are writing, consider whether the term is absolutely essential.

In all these situations, if you have decided to delve into a sensitive or controversial issue, take extra care. Have someone you trust look at your first copy. If something strikes you or that person as "over the top," take it out or rewrite it. Many times you can provoke a positive response from the reader if you rewrite what you are trying to say in a less edgy or more discreet manner. If you don't think you are capable of doing that or if the subject matter doesn't lend itself to a more nuanced approach, consider excising it. The reader wants to know what kind of person you are, but an overly provocative essay—even one needlessly incendiary sentence—can give an impression you may not want to convey and one that you have no ability to correct. Think about it.

Chapter Four

More Advice as You Write

In this chapter, we'll help you with rules—do's and don'ts—we've developed over the years. We learned many of these rules through painful trial and error. We felt the sting of editors' derision and readers' remonstrances. We made dumb mistakes.

So you've settled on a prompt and are set to write a killer admissions essay. No pressure there. Just the rest of your life (not really, see the chapter "What if You Don't Get Your First Choice"). To this we say (and we are quoting Green Bay Packers quarterback Aaron Rodgers here), "**Relax.**"

A strong essay relies on many of the same skills demanded of any other writing: sharp observations, strong analysis, and a deft writing touch. We want to help you avoid common mistakes that sap energy from your writing and confuse readers. In other words, we want to help you avoid a sure way to get your essay tossed on the "Reject pile."

In this chapter and others, you'll find a wide range of advice on grammar, sentence construction, vocabulary, and work habits. These tips aren't just for high schoolers facing admissions essays. These are good for writers of any age who want to write clear, compelling prose. We hope you get into your first-choice school, but whether or not you do, you can use what you learn here. There is always a market for clear writing.

Rule 1: Remember the reader. You must keep the reader engaged.

Often young writers, and some not so young, approach a writing assignment hoping to dazzle the reader with erudition and a sesquipedalian vocabulary. In other words, they're writing to entertain themselves and not engage the reader. Obscure vocabulary, like *sesquipedalian*, may have a place in some pieces, but you should employ these words with caution. You are not writing to entertain yourself or show how clever you can be with long, labyrinthine sentences. *Don't use big words or pretentious phrases you wouldn't use in your everyday conversation and writing. You are writing to communicate with a reader—in this case your admissions reader.*

You're seeking to tell that admissions reader who you are and what you stand for. You're describing your "brand," so to speak. That means you can approach an essay in many different ways, as long as what you write is honest and authentic. You don't have to claim to have saved the world to impress colleges. You just have to be genuine, specific, and focused about who you are and what you want to do on campus. Remember, colleges see lots of applicants with stellar grades and test scores. They're looking for students who will thrive on campus and influence their peers in a positive manner. Show the reader how you will be an asset to the school.

In the case of a college essay, unlike other writing, you don't know anything about the reader, what his or her tastes are, or what he or she is looking for in an essay. Don't try to guess. Just produce something that is true to the way you feel and communicates clearly. There's no bluffing here. College readers, including those who read your essay, can detect insincerity, false bravado, or phony modesty instantly. It rarely takes them more than one hundred words. You can also be sure the admissions reader has waded through thickets of impenetrable writing, attempting to puzzle out a writer's intentions . . . or, more likely, just moved on to the next essay.

Rule 2: Start with something you know, something that's true. And see where it leads. Never make things up.

Truth is important. The reader is trying to ascertain if he or she can trust you, which is a difficult task to convey in an essay. That's why when you are stuck for what to write, write what you are familiar with or what you are passionate about. (And as we said previously if you can't find an opening, start in the middle. Or somewhere else. The point is don't get hung up waiting for the perfect opening sentence.) Your essay has succeeded if the reader can feel your passion—and believes you to be a genuine person.

Rule 3: One thought per sentence.

A common temptation when students are writing their Common App essay is that they lard sentences with clauses, asides, or other commentary—sentences that are hard to follow, that meander. The reader grows confused or frustrated—the "Reject pile" awaits.

Rule 4: Make your sentences tight and bright.

Don't puff up sentences with extraneous words that bog down sentences and exhaust readers. *Avoid words like* very, a bit, somewhat, *and their ilk; they add nothing to a sentence.* Try this: Find any sentence with the word *very* as a modifier. Take it out. Read it again. It's punchier, right? Most modifiers impart little but insecurity or laziness. Every sentence should be muscular and lean. It should propel you to the next sentence.

Rule 5: No throat clearing.

Phrases like "the fact is," or "the question as to whether" or "there is no doubt that" are the equivalent of a writer clearing his or her throat. *Get to the point. Start with action.* Don't back into a story with extraneous background. Grab readers by starting with a compelling scene, thought, or statement. Don't meander. Think of your favorite movies and books. The best scenes don't start with characters spending hours going about their daily routines. They start with a key moment. If your essay is telling a story, make sure you can identify that key moment.

Rule 6: Banish passive voice.

Passive voice is a curse. "Charlie was running down the street." That's a passive way to say "Charlie ran down the street." Another example from the Purdue Writing Lab: "The boy was bitten by the dog." The action is backward. The dog bit the boy.

Passive voice camouflages action and drains drama from your writing. It creates awkward moments and confusion. One of the most infamous passive constructions came from former President Richard Nixon during the Watergate scandal, which forced him to resign from the presidency: "Mistakes were made," he said. Much more effective: "I made a mistake." Avoiding passive voice is a rule that will never go out of style. If you take away nothing else, please take that.

Rule 7: Avoid adverbs. Adverb abuse is rampant.

Strive for simple, clear, and punchy by deleting all but the most vital adverbs. For instance: "Sobbed uncontrollably." Is there any other way to sob? Same with "objected vociferously." How else would you do that? Most adverbs add nothing but deadweight to a sentence. More excellent examples of adverb abuse from kathysteinemann.com: *move softly = tiptoe; drink greedily = guzzle; close loudly = slam.* When your Common App essay is a couple of words over the 650-word limit look for those pesky adverbs. Omitting them is a great way of getting your essay down to the word limit without affecting the quality or your message.

Rule 8: Department of Redundancy Department.

Don't repeat yourself. Draft a brief outline of the points you want to make. That will help you organize your thoughts and avoid repetition of thoughts or phrases. Also, don't use the same word repeatedly to describe an action or event. *Find synonyms.* A general rule is avoid using the same verb, adverb, or adjective twice in the same paragraph and no more than three times in the entire essay (it may be harder to do with nouns, especially if they are the subject of your essay). Even then, try not to use the same word more than once if you can help it.

Rule 9: Take care to find the best word.

The best word is not necessarily the first word that comes to mind. You can write: He was tired. Or you can write: He was exhausted. Which is more compelling? Quite often you will write "tired" but when you go back to edit, you will say to yourself, "I'm not sure about *tired.* Is there a better word?" That's why it is important to use a thesaurus, either online or, if you're really in a pinch, a real book. Either way, find the right word. The French writer Gustave Flaubert (*Madame Bovary*) coined a term for exactly the right word. He called it *le mot juste* (remember, the first time you use a foreign expression, italicize it).

Rule 10: Specific images compel; generics don't.

Your writing comes from your observation of the world. Use those observations, no matter how tiny, to paint a scene with words. *Show, don't tell.* Setting a scene visually can be powerful.

Rule 11: Endings count.

A lot. A powerful ending can compensate for many shortcomings. You don't need to summarize, but you should leave the reader with something visceral, a thought, an emotion, or an insight into your character and experience.

Remember: **Rules are important but not sacrosanct.** It's OK if you dangle a participle once in a while, as long as it is crucial to the point you're making. If your editors pick it out, consider changing it. Other people sometimes see what you can't.

Some Final Thoughts

Don't write when you're tired. Few people are able to write well when they are bleary-eyed. Same goes for writing under the influence of alcohol or other substances. Better to get some sleep and approach your work fresh. That means in the morning—don't procrastinate. Get to it.

Take a break if you're stuck. Take a bike ride, a walk, anything to get blood pumping. That allows your subconscious to work on the dilemma. You'll be surprised how often this works. We know many writers who find their best ideas on walks or bike rides.

Keep at it. A first draft is not a final draft. It's a start. Ernest Hemingway said, "The only writing is rewriting," and who are we to argue?

Your first draft is just that, a draft. It won't, shouldn't, and can't be the final product. Give yourself time to edit and refine and to show it to people you trust.

Be fearless. Don't be afraid to toss it out and start again. Yes, start over. Save the earlier draft, print it out, and tuck it in a drawer. Sit back, take a deep breath, and reimagine. You'll be surprised how effective this is. Writers can get stuck in a rut, particularly if their first sentences lead them down a path that is not productive. You can spend a lot of time trying to fix it or you can just start over. We advise the latter. Trust your instincts here. If you think the piece is stilted or awkward or just disingenuous, it is. Talk it out with the outside editor—friend, parent, or teacher—you trust. Then try again if it doesn't work.

Chapter Five

The Prompts and Some Illustrative Essays

Based on the results of the Common App survey, the 2020–2021 prompts are likely to be the same or at least similar for the next couple of years. Here are some suggestions that might help when you are considering what to write.

Some students have a background, identity, interest, or talent that is so meaningful they believe their application would be incomplete without it. If this sounds like you, then please share your story.

Many students develop effective essays by discussing their heritage. If your parents or grandparents come from disparate backgrounds and have different traditions or customs, the influence that has had on you growing up can make for an interesting story. Along those lines, you might write an entertaining tale about where you or your family originally came from—the rural South, the inner-city, or a foreign country. Likewise, if you have an unusual hobby, passion, or skill, you can write about that. But remember, the essay is not primarily about your family traditions, background, or hobby—you must explain what those things tell the reader about you. Be authentic. *Tip: If you are writing about a talent, skill, or interest you developed at an early age, you should develop your essay around how it is related to your high school years. Don't dwell on your early years.*

I was in a new city, surrounded by a new team, competing in a new sport for my first time. Needless to say, I was distressed. My nerves took over, making me sick. I had learned to bench press only a mere three weeks before, and I was the lone female sophomore on the team. Why did I put myself in this situation? Two months earlier I was participating in preseason strength and conditioning with my softball team, when Coach Adams, the strength and conditioning coach, approached me randomly. First, he commented on my great squat form, then he asked me if I had any interest in powerlifting. Did I want to compete with the powerlifting team at Nationals? I agreed, without hesitation, because primarily I am a competitor. Little did I know that I had made a life-changing decision.

I worried everyday about this decision. I was terrified of competing by myself. I felt so unprepared, and I thought I might let everyone down. My softball season that year was, to say the least, underwhelming with a total of two wins, so I focused my energy and competitive drive on learning the skills for powerlifting. I fell in love with my newfound skills and the rewards it brought: powerlifting gave me confidence.

After growing up in three different countries and struggling to find where I fit in, having Coach Adams believe in me from the start meant a lot. To have that consistent support from the outset was an emotional relief that I had not felt anywhere else. Over the next two months, I trained by myself and started attending powerlifting club meetings. What I loved as much as the lifting was the community aspect of the club. Everyone was a part of a team with a common goal. Yet as I grew more comfortable with Coach Adams and the powerlifting club, I became concerned I might let them down. I'm a people pleaser, and these people had made me feel so at home in such a short time it would be devastating if I failed. The night before the trip to Nationals I never felt more alone.

I remember the ride to the airport vividly. I cried to my mom about how nervous I was. Every time my family moved to a different country, I experienced similar feelings but this time the nervousness and vulnerability felt worse. When we arrived in Oklahoma, weigh-ins were delayed. People were freaking out about not making weight. We all hung out and waited together. This was a small gesture, but to be accepted by the upperclassmen meant everything to me and helped ease my nerves.

I was the last person competing when it was my turn for the final deadlift. Deadlift is my favorite lift and it gives me a feeling like nothing else. I attempted a weight I had never even thought about trying before. I stepped up onto stage, shaking, and saw the whole team cheering for me. It hit me that it was worth it all; I had made a new family. My teammates' support empowered me, and I lifted the weight with ease. I immediately ran over and hugged my coach. The satisfaction of making a new PR in

> deadlift was unmatched. The difference one team and coach made in my life is always something I will hold close to my heart, and it will guide me, as I make my way through adult life.
>
> Powerlifting is not just a sport for me, it is a place where I can finally fit in, especially after being continually relocated. After Nationals, I assumed a leadership role in the club. I became more personable and learned a philosophy that I couldn't get anywhere else. These skills transferred over into every aspect of my life, and I can honestly say that I am a different and better person now.

This is a wonderful essay. The writer never treads too close to cliché by using the relative novelty of being a female powerlifter (notice she does not dwell on the fact she is female in her essay). That would be an obvious approach, but not necessarily an effective one. Nor does she dwell on the outcome of what happened at Nationals—we learn she achieved her personal record but we don't find out how her team did—because it's not germane to the story. What she emphasizes is what any good Common App essay should: how it changed her and made her a better person; the team cheering for her and her discovery she had a new family; the difference her team and her coach made in her life; how she became more personable and learned a philosophy. The small details about how nervous she was, the drive to the airport, and the weigh-ins are just right. She adds them to give color to the story but she doesn't belabor them: not too much, not too little. If you decide to select this prompt and you have an experience like hers, this is a good model.

> When I was younger, family and friends gave me diaries as gifts. Now, dozens of books fill my shelves, except most only carry empty pages. On Christmas of my freshman year, I received a small leather book titled "Favorite Moment a Day." Maybe it was the books in my room filled with lost potential, or the fact that I'd just started what everyone told me were the four most memorable years of my life that sparked a newfound fear: forgetting who I am now when I'm older. The idea of one day not remembering my dance recitals, sixteenth birthday, or favorite songs in high school seemed scary enough that I couldn't risk losing a part of them.
>
> Determined to take this journal seriously, on December twenty-eighth, I wrote my first entry: my family drove through northern Michigan into the town of Petoskey where my grandparents live. Through the droplet-speckled window, holiday lights covered the pines as we returned to my home away from home.

The "Favorite Moment a Day" journal quickly became a space to write everything down. It followed my life for the next year as I pressed dried rose petals from the corsage of my first high school dance and taped a torn Jack Johnson concert ticket to its pages. My family watched me take life in through words as I filled that first journal, and soon my mom bought my next journal. I searched more, observing the things and people around me. Sinking into the cushions of my cousin's couch, I held his daughter for the first time. My aunt watched nearby, bearing an uncanny resemblance to my late grandmother. Through my writing I realized four generations of my family were visible that afternoon and how lucky I am to have them.

Some moments, though, take more than observation. Journaling proved to be a necessity as it was no longer just how I remembered things, but how I understood them. Moments in my life that are too hard to say aloud, or too personal to share, I save for paper and pen. During my sophomore year, my brother was severely depressed. Throughout his recovery, I lost touch with my own happiness, but felt selfish in my struggle. Day by day, page by page, our family healed. And through their love, friends' support, and processing it all through asking and answering my own questions, I healed, too. Life's tougher moments lay enclosed in my journals, shielding them from eyes that aren't my own.

But for each page of hardship, there are dozens of happy ones. In journaling, I've learned to pick out the simple moments that spark inspiration. High Five Choir, a musical group for students of all abilities, connects peers through music and raises disability awareness. Each day, I spend forty minutes with some of my best friends and I'm reminded of how much good exists. Jenna is twenty-one with the sassiest comebacks but the sweetest heart. When I met her a year ago, she asked me what I love to do. I answered, "Dance." She taught me "dance" in sign language, and now, whenever we see each other, we sign the word like it's our little secret.

After three years, I still write often, but my fear has somewhat subsided. I've realized if you focus too much on capturing the future, you miss out on the now. On a wintry drive into northern Michigan, I found my favorite moment of the day. But now, these moments find me. A particularly vibrant sunset or times I laugh until I cry are mixed into observations, questions, and defining moments. Writing is therapeutic, poetic, and meaningful. It's hilarious and sometimes embarrassing to notice my immaturity, but prideful to see my growth, and the understanding that my growth is just beginning. Journaling is no longer how I remember my life, but part of how I live it.

This is a nice reflective essay about keeping a diary. The writer takes important moments from her life and describes them in a way that really shows the reader about her personality. After reading this piece, you not only get a picture of what kind of person she is but you can also see how she has learned about herself. The line "but now these moments find me" is especially effective. There is a minor technical problem with this essay: the word "prideful" in the last paragraph is misused. Prideful, while meaning proud, generally connotes excessive pride, even to the point of arrogance, which is not what the writer intends to convey (and in some sense is the opposite of what the writer wants to say about herself). The sentence would read better as "It's hilarious and sometimes embarrassing to notice my immaturity, but I am proud to see how I've grown and realize I am just beginning." Many college readers are willing to overlook this type of misused word because they want the student's "true voice." However, we believe this is one of those situations where a careful edit can make the piece clearer and even better.

The lessons we take from obstacles we encounter can be fundamental to later success. Recount a time when you faced a challenge, setback, or failure. How did it affect you, and what did you learn from the experience?

The point of this "adversity prompt" is to emphasize your personal growth, rather than the specific setback you encountered. Students commonly concentrate too much on the obstacle or hardship and not enough on how they learned from it. There are other pitfalls in this prompt. Some students want to write about the first time they got a bad grade. It's hard to craft an interesting essay about a bad grade you received and how it made you a better student, unless it contains an interesting hook, like a teacher who inspired you. Essays on athletic injuries that derailed your career or a relative who suffered an illness can be effective, but you must emphasize the positive rather than dwelling on the negative. Whatever the challenge or setback, this is a good prompt to show the reader you are a resilient person. *Tip: It is OK to be vulnerable. Vulnerability can show strength. The strength comes from how you react to the situation. Make sure not to overshare the adversity of your story. This prompt is also about risk. High school students hear about risk all the time. They are encouraged to "take risks," but what does that mean? Smart risks, not foolish ones. Rule of thumb: Is this something you would tell someone on your first meeting with them?*

January 19th, 2018, will be the first annual Penguin Awareness Day at my high school. Designated students will greet all 2,000 pupils with smiles and penguin stickers as they enter school. I was responsible for putting together Penguin Awareness Day, in the hope the effort will be worth it if we brighten even one student's day. Why did I do this?

It started freshman year when I was captain of our undefeated freshman football team. In our last game with tensions running high, something happened to me. After the game when I got on the bus, my coach noticed I was staring at him blankly, and he sent me to the hospital. I don't remember it, but apparently during the game I sustained a concussion.

Most concussions resolve quickly, but mine lasted five months—the absolute worst period of my life. I constantly felt foggy, had throbbing headaches, and my balance was off. Everything was hazy, and I couldn't distinguish reality from dreams. To make matters worse, my beloved grandfather suddenly passed away, and I was devastated. He was the one person I could always talk to about anything.

Because I couldn't concentrate, my grades slipped. I lost my passion for playing the piano, my way of escaping life's problems and living in the moment. I had enjoyed the piano since I was four years old, and now it was gone.

My symptoms eventually subsided, and I regained my ability to focus. I stopped feeling helpless and began to realize I could be happy again. But it was up to me. The outcome of the struggles I faced was the next chapter of my story.

Two years later, I now believe that surviving my post-concussive symptoms has shaped me into the person I am today. During my miserable period, I learned much about myself and others. By speaking with other teens with similar issues, I learned that everybody has a story, and I decided not to judge people quickly before hearing their stories. I have become more sensitive to others' problems and struggles. It's important to hear their perspective.

The pain of losing my grandfather made me understand the importance of family. I realize how fortunate I am to have a loving family, something that didn't occur to me much in my younger years.

Between the times of sorrow and pain, I learned that the small acts of kindness people showed me are what count. I always make sure to stay levelheaded. Stressing over the small stuff is never worth it—just appreciate the little things and never take anything for granted. I've come out of my shell, become more open, and less afraid of what others think.

Two years after my concussion, I think my personality can be summed up basically in two words: compassionate and happy. My positive attitude is a direct result of the time I spent in a negative place. I always try to send out positive vibes by doing things like wearing goofy clothes or anonymously slipping notes in peoples' lockers that say, "Have an amazing day! ♡" I want to make people smile.

I think of myself as perseverant, and I am on a mission—to add some happiness to a stressful school environment. Whether it is complimenting someone or having a memorial for lost socks, I want to brighten somebody's day. I don't want to see others in the position I was in, and it makes me happy to see them happy, especially if I've played a role.

I took my mission to Student Senate, where I came up with the idea for Penguin Awareness Day and other initiatives. My experience has made me more perceptive—just because people look fine doesn't mean they are not going through tough times. And when you come to school, getting a penguin sticker just might make you feel a little better.

One bit of advice students receive is that they should make their essays unique (but not "very unique"; see chapter nine, "Special Usage Rules II," p. 88). Unfortunately, it's not always easy to make your essay unique, especially if it is a "challenge to overcome" essay. When students write about a health challenge, they often detail a sports injury and the response can be predictable—initial depression, a long period of recovery, and finally a return to competition. Nothing unique about that, and college readers must go through hundreds of similar essays. This essay could easily have turned out the same way and, in fact, it skirts the edges of the predictable. However, the writer actually did something unique by creating "Penguin Awareness Day," and it turns a mundane essay into a memorable one. The other lesson here is to avoid making your essay depressing. Essays about injuries can quickly turn dismal, and a reader is likely to stop reading a dismal essay. It's true every student won't have as good a story as this one but no matter what challenge you overcome, try to tell your story in an uplifting fashion. That's what this writer did with his penguin story (which he later crafted into his valedictory graduation speech). One of the interesting things is why the writer chose penguins. He doesn't give the reason, which makes the essay more intriguing. It leaves a reader wondering about the writer, and that makes it stand out.

Clean tights and dirty floors are the mantra of the ballet world. As a child, you see only the clean, pink tights hugging a ballerina's perfectly sculpted legs under a sea of bright stage lights. But as you grow up you see the dirty floors and futile quest for perfection. Thriving in an atmosphere of grit, zeal, and sacrifice, I've never been afraid of dirt. However, the promise of achievement isn't necessarily the ultimate goal.

Crammed in a musty room with 80 dancers seeking acceptance into Boston Ballet's Summer Dance Program, I shared my space at the barre with my younger sister, Laura. After the audition, an instructor approached my sister, whose face lit up. She smiled and squealed with delight, "The lady said she would try to get me a scholarship to go this summer!"

"Oh my gosh, Laura, congrats. That's awesome," I exclaimed, trying hard to match her level of excitement.

Although my sister and I are very close and I was happy for her, it was hard not to feel jealous. It was even more difficult to hide my disappointment when I received notification the following month I was rejected from Boston Ballet's Summer Intensive. My little sister was not only good enough to attend, but good enough to receive a scholarship. At family gatherings, Laura, who merely considered ballet fun and a casual activity, would announce she had been admitted into the program and I would have to admit that I had not. I, who arrived half an hour early before every class to warm up and kept a dance journal tracking my goals and progress.

Back then, my value and self-worth were so wrapped up in my achievements as a dancer, I felt that if I failed, my identity would be stripped away. Were all the sacrifices I made to pursue a professional career worth it? Would I ever be good enough? How did something that brought me so much joy turn into constant self-criticism and pressure?

I was utterly embarrassed and totally devastated. My inner core was rattled and torn. If I wasn't good enough to get into Boston's program, would I ever be good enough to go professional? Why did my sister, who never took dance as seriously as I did, get in while I hadn't?

After feeling sorry for myself, I returned to class. My mind was clear and open. I recognized I had to return to the roots of why I originally started dancing. On the dirty, shoe-scuffed floors stood a girl who smiled for the first time in a long time. This was my moment; I decided to make the most of it. Living in the moment felt as freeing as leaping into the sky. With this freedom came improvement. Instead of worrying about the placement of every tendon and ligament, I landed a triple pirouette effortlessly. I marveled at the moment without worrying about the next audition.

Being denied from Boston Ballet's Summer Intensive was the best thing that could have happened to me. I learned what truly brings happiness is not necessarily quantifiable achievement. Becoming too focused on success, I lost the happiness I first found in dance. I had been continually chasing success, ultimately an unfulfilling endeavor.

This experience prepared me to lose a close race for Student Council Vice President. It was a little embarrassing, but not devastating. I recognized there would be other opportunities in the future and I refused to be defined by failure.

Ironically, I saw the tangible results of this mindset the next year when I was accepted into Boston Ballet's Summer Intensive and elected Secretary of Student Council. There is an element of luck, whether it is acceptance into dance programs or winning an election. I learned it is a mistake to get too consumed in your achievements. You must have a more well-rounded perspective about who you are.

This is a great example of something mentioned elsewhere—failure can be a more compelling story than success. This story is really about the futile quest for perfection and learning about yourself. The third paragraph from the end is especially strong—you want to read that over carefully. (In fact, the final two paragraphs are almost anticlimactic, but not quite.) There is also a story within a story (this is known as a "frame narrative"): the writer's relationship with her sister. That makes the piece even more readable. Writing this essay made the writer more introspective.

Reflect on a time when you questioned or challenged a belief or idea. What prompted your thinking? What was the outcome?

Students who choose this prompt usually feel passionate about a belief they have questioned or challenged. This often makes for a strong essay because you can demonstrate your passion about your subject to the reader. These essays tend to come from the heart; they are sincere. There is a potential hazard, namely, that if you are writing about a controversial subject, your reader might not agree with your position. That doesn't mean you should not take a stand in your essay, but you should avoid the trap of coming off as dogmatic or arrogant, an easy trap to fall into. When you write this essay, your skill will be obvious if you can show yourself as committed to your convictions but reasonable in your approach. *Tip: Don't write an essay where you are questioning something that is illegal, like drug use or alcohol. For instance, don't write about why you think the drinking age should be lowered to eighteen. It might sound self-serving and that you are trying to justify illegal behavior.*

Throughout my life, I've always felt it is important to stand up for what I believe. Although this sounds like a cliché, I can say that one of my strengths is that I truly live by that statement.

An example of this took place when I lived in Korea and attended Seoul Foreign School (SFS), an international school with firm Christian beliefs, which required all the teachers to be Christian. One day in advisory, my adviser was discussing religion. She asked everyone in the class to raise their hands if they believed in evolution. My classmates looked indifferent to the question, as if just the thought of answering "yes" to this question was alien to them. After a moment of self-conscious hesitation, I raised my hand. My adviser looked at me, almost incredulously, and started asking me questions.

"So," she said in a mocking tone, "if you believe in evolution, you believe that if I gave it enough time, this water bottle could turn into this folder?"

I stammered, "No, of course not, and attempted to justify my position to her. However, I was caught off-guard, and it was difficult to stand up to my teacher in front of my whole class. She made it uncomfortable for me and I could tell she was trying to make me look silly. But I stood my ground, and refused to back down. I did not argue but I made my point respectfully. It makes me angry looking back on how my teacher treated me, but I am also proud that, even at that age, I was able to stand up for myself. I think it speaks to who I am as a person that I stood my ground and didn't succumb to her when she started making fun of my beliefs.

This adviser was dogmatic about her beliefs and would not listen to other viewpoints. She refused to understand that people have different opinions and not everyone shares the same views she does. That particular day always comes to mind when I recall the times that I have stood up for my beliefs.

I'm not an extremely extroverted person, but when I see someone belittling me or another person's values, I don't hesitate to defend myself and others, no matter what. If I don't agree with how I or someone else is being treated, I will not be passive about it. It's easy to go through life not making your voice heard, but I have found that you feel more empowered as a person when you stand up for yourself and for others, regardless of how people may react. This has served me well in many different situations and I am glad I possess this characteristic.

It was daunting to speak up in front of my whole class, none of whom agreed with me, but I have no regrets. It is important in life to be confident in your values and proud of what you stand for, and this is a quality of mine that I hope to take with me as I go through the world.

This is an excellent answer to a prompt that students are often reluctant to select. At 520 words, it is concise, clear, and direct. In the last paragraph she ties an incident that happened to her years ago to her personality today. She is telling the school things about herself that the school would not otherwise know from her resume. That's an important aspect of the Common App essay.

Describe a problem you've solved or a problem you'd like to solve. It can be an intellectual challenge, a research query, an ethical dilemma—anything that is of personal importance, no matter the scale. Explain its significance to you and what steps you took or could be taken to identify a solution.

This "problem-solving" essay is the one where you may be able to write about something unique because your problem may be one no one else has ever imagined writing about before. It can be trivial or it can be serious, just be sure to concentrate on why the problem is important to you and how you will solve it. Also, don't take on more than you can handle. Suppose you select a global problem like the coronavirus or climate change. You should consider several things: Many students are likely to write about it, and it is a complicated topic. It can be difficult to explain your solution and tell much about yourself in the allotted word count. You can still write about climate change but consider limiting your essay to giving your take on some specific aspect of climate change. *Tip: It is easy to overload this essay with facts and have it become a research paper at the expense of your story. Keep your facts to a bare minimum.*

"Persuade your neighbors to compromise whenever you can"—Abraham Lincoln, 1850

I have always been interested in current events—sports, politics, international news, pop culture, and everything in between. As I have matured and I routinely check the news on a variety of different sites, I have been exposed to a greater range of articles and stories, and politics has taken center stage.

I should have seen this coming. When I was in grade school, I memorized the order of the presidents of the United States before I understood anything about domestic or foreign policy. Simultaneously, from my parents and teachers, I learned certain core values such as respect, honesty, and listening before understanding their importance. These values have been ingrained in me since I was little, and now I realize the critical role they play in society. However, I have come to realize that American politicians exhibit few of the key values that I hold so dear.

As someone who has followed elections for years, I care deeply about the past, present, and future of this country, and hope that America can change its current divisive trajectory. Our Founding Fathers envisioned a country based on the principles of a republic, where power is vested in the people, who express that power through their elected representatives. Today's America has deviated from those goals, and my generation's dilemma will be to reunite the country based on the core values it was founded on and the values my parents instilled in me. While it is naïve to expect a perfect government based on grade school morals, our country must attempt to get started.

Our politicians must learn to disagree without being disagreeable. Every American has the fundamental right to his or her own opinion, but I am wary of the future when our politicians continue to disagree about every issue just to spite their opposition. However, there are ways to unite our ideologically divided country, and they begin with the values I take pride in. Each party fiercely blocks every piece of legislation, criticizes every speech, and undermines everything said or done by the opposition. Instead, politicians should listen to each other, analyze the specifics they disagree with, and try to work together to get both sides what they want.

When compromise is impossible on a particular issue, then I believe the best approach is to step back, take a break, and try to compromise later. Understandably, the world's pressing problems cannot always wait for compromise. But when politicians slander each other on national television simply because they disagree about something trivial, this only widens the gap between the two sides and exacerbates the problem. When leaders display their stubbornness, their followers emulate them. If I were to become a politician, which has always been a possible goal of mine, I would defend my ideological positions, but I would always strive to be honest and morally sound. While morals don't always win elections, my generation's collective morals can help start this trend.

Overall, American citizens must take a step back, examine each issue, and imagine not only what they want in a perfect world, but also what they would settle for. If everyone, male and female, rich and poor, black and white, urban and rural, cannot find some common ground on the

> issues standing in the way of national unity, our country's future looks grim. However, I believe in my heart that every American can put differences aside to encourage our leaders to do what is morally right. While each person has a unique set of beliefs, which makes doing what is "morally right" even more complicated, there are some morals that everyone can agree with. I know that I can exhibit good morals, and I hope my values can be of some help to the future of our country, in the spirit of compromise and kindness Abraham Lincoln advocated.

The best thing about this well-done essay, both in its tone and its message, is that it is not strident. The writer could have easily lapsed in a dogmatic political diatribe, which might reflect badly on him and turn off the reader. Rather, he takes a calm and measured approach. The reader should come off with a good impression of him. Notice also how he introduces his essay with a quote (it's a good approach, but only if you can find an appropriate quote) by Lincoln in this case, and he circles back to it effectively in his conclusion. That stylistic point, when done well, usually strengthens your conclusion.

Discuss an accomplishment, event, or realization that sparked a period of personal growth and a new understanding of yourself or others.

The key to this essay is usually telling the story of acquiring newfound maturity. It can be where you describe a volunteer project, a summer job, a vacation, or a competition—athletic, dance, music, speech, or scientific—anything that made you a more mature person. Helping other people, interacting with others in a work setting, or winning and losing can all be character builders. Don't make the mistake of confusing this with your resume—that's where detailed descriptions of your volunteer projects and awards belong. Where you finish in a competition is not important here; the details of how you competed are. This essay is to show the way those things have helped you grow and understand yourself better. *Tip: Stay away from bar mitzvahs, confirmations, winning state championships, and so on, unless you can find a special take on them. They have been done to death. Don't use the phrase "I will always remember this" or its equivalent, "I will remember this all my life." Clichés.*

"The Chinese government is coming to take you away!"

While it's fairly normal for siblings to exchange petty insults like "Mom and Dad love me more," and "I wish you were never born," my older sister's taunts were strangely political.

As little girls living temporarily in China with our parents, we were both acutely aware of the country's strict one-child policy, but somehow my sister terrorized me into thinking my mere existence was a crime.

The Chinese government never came to take me away, but I did internalize a sensitivity to abandonment from a very young age. I knew that hundreds of Chinese babies, especially girls, were discarded in alleys and trash cans every day.

Walking the polluted streets of Qingdao with my mom one afternoon, I remember spotting a gaunt girl with sunken cheeks holding a cardboard sign with the words 没有家 or "no home" written in chicken scratch. My mom ushered me along the sidewalk, but as I turned my head, I felt her eyes glued to me, silently screaming "Take me home!"

From that moment on, the idea of adopting a younger sister dominated my thoughts. I imagined becoming a hero and molding this lost little person into an amazing human being. So, two years later, when our family moved back to Chicago, I formally launched my relentless adoption campaign, printing pictures and biographies of little girls who needed a home until my parents were completely on board. In 2013, after years of excessive forms, permits, and waitlists, our family finally received the call about Kiara, a four-year-old foster child from the South Side of Chicago. We eventually learned that Kiara had suffered horrific physical and emotional abuse, but it was years before I fully understood the depth of her trauma.

Almost immediately after her arrival, Kiara and I became locked in an ongoing power struggle. With Kiara mired in behavioral issues, I was constantly trying to control everything she did and felt frustrated by her inability to listen. After months of door slamming and stuff grabbing, the friction between us became unbearable. I realized I had to pull back and discard the naïve, big-sister rescue fantasy I'd constructed in my head. I realized I couldn't singlehandedly erase or heal Kiara's problems. I could only be her older sister, day in and day out, building love and trust over time with small acts of sisterhood, like sitting in the front row of her school plays and french braiding her hair every morning. It was putting aside my homework to deejay her weekend modeling performances so she could strut down the hallway "catwalk" between our rooms, wearing my clothes.

Last summer, when the day finally arrived to legally adopt Kiara, my family headed downtown to the courthouse, feeling nervous and excited.

With Kiara's sweaty hand wrapped snuggly in mine, I could sense her fear. I sent her three squeezes, our secret handshake, and Kiara's deep dark eyes looked up at me as if to silently say "I love you, too."

The judge glanced around the barren courtroom. Sensing Kiara's hesitation, the judge asked a simple, get-to-know-you about siblings. Usually, when prompted with this question, Kiara would chatter excitedly about her nine half-siblings, all born to the same mom, but with six different dads. This time, Kiara told the judge she only had two older sisters, one who lets her sit in the front seat and the other who plays songs with *swears* in them. Reaching up and locking her fingers with mine, Kiara squeezed my hand three times, sending me a secret but undeniable message: we're not perfect, but we're family.

I now know that when it comes right down to it, an older sister doesn't have to be a hero or even an amazing role model; sometimes, she's just a hand to hold.

This piece illustrates how an effective essay can come from a good story. The opening quote grabs the reader and helps set up the story, actually two stories. If there is a criticism of this piece, it is the writer could have made the transition between the two stories smoother. The older sister gets lost in the second story; it might have been better had she earned a mention. But these are small points. The essay does a good job of holding the reader's attention, and the ending is excellent. Perhaps the writer's older sister should get a follow-up mention, but the touching portrayal of Kiara more than makes up for it. One effective strategy is telling the reader about yourself through your relationship with another person. In a few sentences, the writer does a masterful job of telling the reader about Kiara—and about herself as well. The essay is supposed to be about you, but when you can tell the reader about yourself through another person, as she does here, it's often quite successful. Granted, not everyone can write about growing up in one-child Communist China, but the writer takes advantage of her personal story. *(Note: The Common App may not accept foreign language and other special characters.)*

At 14, I stood in the back corner of the room, quivering at the sight of the beautiful, confident dancers wearing extravagant hairstyles and neon crop tops that highlighted their well-defined stomach muscles. I had abandoned my rigid dance studio for the summer intensive of Lisa Douglas, whom I had admired for years. But as I looked around, I knew I was in over my head.

After several days, I started growing comfortable with the new dances—contemporary styles and movements that challenged me physically and mentally. However, I still feared being judged by the talented dancers around me. On the final day, Lisa Douglas watched me in my hiding place. When the music stopped, she asked me to perform in front of everyone. With nerves jangling, I performed onstage. Minutes later, there was a roar of applause and the formerly intimidating dancers shouted words of praise. That moment changed my attitude, providing me confidence to perform and confirming that my hard work was paying off.

I fell in love with dance when I was three, and it gradually continued to boost my spirits, giving me escape from stressful nights when my mind would race wildly. For fifteen years, the joy of movement, release of tension, and satisfaction resulting from my efforts kept me coming to class every week for hours on end.

But that was internally; externally, it was different. As a freshman, I was riddled with insecurities; I dreaded the spotlight for fear of being judged. At the back of class, I worked hard but avoided attention. However, this insecure mindset was impractical for someone aspiring to become an accomplished dancer.

After my experience in Ms. Douglas's class, I entered a world of competition designed to expose my vulnerability and lack of confidence. My new teachers encouraged me to confront uncomfortable experiences. The first small steps were standing in front of class or demonstrating an exercise to everyone. Eventually, my confidence grew, and I began accepting more demanding challenges. I agreed to partnering classes, where I was swept off my feet by college-level male dancers, and was thrown into improv circles, forced to make humiliating animal noises in front of strangers.

Soon, my instructors began dragging me to public auditions. At first, these auditions were epic failures: I would forget choreography, stumble over my feet, and freeze during the improvisation section. However, the embarrassment in front of experienced dancers pushed me to change my approach to auditions. I had to figure ways to increase my confidence.

Fortunately, my enthusiasm for dance was growing. I was proud of learning to manage my time more efficiently. As high school work ramped up, my work ethic and dedication were tested. Spending 20+ hours at the studio and then coming home to hours of homework was mentally exhausting, but I was managing it all.

Besides the injuries, getting cut from auditions, endurance issues and exhaustion, the competitive world of dance presents a continuing challenge because of the constant comparison with others and the resulting self-doubt. Dance taught me to focus on my own improvement rather than obsessing over other dancers. I started applying this approach to my school career, paying less attention to my academic "competition" and concentrating on my personal development.

Throughout my dance and school careers, my resilience has increased and my failures have helped me grow. I perform with a joy that reminds me of the feeling I got when I was three. I overcame many self-imposed obstacles, and I now am a stronger person physically and mentally. I see now, more than ever, how the lessons I learned from dance have carried over into my personal life. I have more confidence in class, a better work ethic in school, and I respond to failure in a positive manner. Every day, I thank my years of dance and my experience with Lisa Douglas's class for my personal development.

Beautiful essay. You can almost envision her gaining confidence. Notice how she sets up her answer to the prompt—this is one of the few times you'll see that it is better not to answer the prompt immediately (and she does answer it in the second paragraph). The story that introduces her to the reader is perfect in illustrating her personal development. It was much better than had she started with "dance increased my confidence . . ." and then told her story. Also notice how there is no mention of any particular successful dance competition. Dance is only the backdrop; the story is really about her. When you are writing your essay, keep that in mind.

Describe a topic, idea, or concept you find so engaging that it makes you lose all track of time. Why does it captivate you? What or who do you turn to when you want to learn more?

The things that captivate you tell the reader about you and your motivation. This is a fairly straightforward prompt, and in some respects it is similar to the first prompt. Except that this prompt requires you to go into further detail about your interest—how you acquired it, how you pursue it, and any mentors you might have. You might talk about your musical interests, interests in art or architecture, business, science, fashion, the environment, and the like. This gives the reader some indication of your intellectual and academic curiosity. *Tip: If you want to demonstrate your intellectual curiosity, it's probably not a good idea to write about binge-watching Netflix. If you want to write about something like playing video games, be sure to make it compelling.*

The Big Cheese

One crisp afternoon after cross-country practice, I sidled into the weight room. I drank in the metallic clinks of the iron plates, the enormous linemen, their torn shirts smeared with textual inspiration. "NEXT BREATH," they told me. "LION PRIDE," they screamed. In the midst of this bedlam, a small voice whispered in my ear, "How much do you like cheese?"

Let's back up. I'm very involved in my school. I'm the guy who runs meetings, scribbles outrageous plans on blackboards, calls, speaks, builds. People come to me, and I help them. But cheese?

I wheeled around, and leaning on a rusting machine was Mr. Cooley, a history teacher. Cooley is a renaissance man, and a fabulously eccentric one at that. I always pictured him as a youngster on Christmas Eve, praying Santa would bring him that anthology of French poetry or that *killer* make-your-own cold fusion kit he had his eye on, and maybe, *just maybe,* if he got lucky, there would be some glass tins of caviar clinking sweetly together at the bottom of his alpaca wool stocking.

Cooley stood there, waiting for my answer. I cautiously spoke up, "Well, I do love my Camembert . . ." Before I could continue, he cut in—"Fabulous. Just what I wanted to hear." He easily read the confusion in my face. "Here's the beef—I'm thinking of starting the Cheese Club. I'm looking for *fromage* enthusiasts like yourself. Whaddya think?" I paused. Cooley is a man whom I respect deeply. He is an athlete, a scholar, a gentleman. Initial shock aside, this might be something I would like. I nodded my affirmation, and replied, "I'll noodle it over."

That night, I indeed pondered the bond between myself and cheese. Cooley chose me because he knew I was eccentric enough, bold enough, *crazy* enough to put myself out on the limb and say, "I'm the president of Cheese Club!" I would take to the halls, posting bills, crying, "Stilton Saturday! Bring your own wheel, and bring a friend!" Suddenly, I smelt an idea. I tip-toed upstairs, pilfered a dusty volume from my mom's library of cookbooks, and slid it into my backpack for tomorrow.

The next morning, I stopped by the social studies department. Each teacher is a busy bee with their own honeycomb, a personal hexagon sporting scale models of the Coliseum and bumper stickers wondering "Iowa—Is This Heaven?" A life-sized bust of Aristotle frowned at me in his pensive way as I walked up to Cooley's desk. He did a full three spins on his desk chair before he came to rest, looking up at me. "Yes?" "I slept on the whole Cheese Club thing, and I have this for you." I unzipped my bag and whipped out my mother's copy of *A Cheese Primer*. Its girth registered a resounding *smack* on the desk, with enough gusto to send Aristotle himself wobbling on his thin marble pedestal. Cooley looked from the book to Aristotle to me, and nodded silently. "Profound," he breathed. Our eyes met, and Cheese Club was born.

A nice, humorous essay that shows that you don't have to use all 650 words to create a good piece. This one is only 511 words, but it accomplishes its goal. The writer might have used his last 140 words to give us some follow-up to what happened with the Cheese Club, but he may have felt this was as far as he could go with this idea—don't pad unnecessarily. (Common App essays don't have to be 650 words, but you can rarely make the impression you want in fewer than 400 words.) This essay gives you a sense of the author and his relationship with his teacher, who has obviously made a lasting impression on him. There is no challenge or setback that was overcome here, but the writer has still accomplished something by creating a new club. The essay is light and breezy, never too serious. A piece like this can also satisfy any number of prompts. It is a good illustration that you don't have to take the prompt or the assignment too seriously. In fact, if you do, sometimes you come up with a ponderous, unreadable essay. It's not bad to lighten up.

Share an essay on any topic of your choice. It can be one you've already written, one that responds to a different prompt, or one of your own design.

We generally discourage students from selecting this prompt. You can usually tailor your topic of choice to one of the other six prompts. Consider what you want to write about and see how it fits with another prompt; the first prompt—background, identity, interest, talent—usually works. If you decide to select this prompt, understand that is both easier and harder than the others. Easier, because it does not require that you answer a question, but harder in that you must provide your own theme. If you choose to write an essay of your choice or you decide to design your own prompt, demonstrate focus in delivering your message; *the Common App essay is not just a creative writing exercise.* Tell the reader something about yourself that is not in your application.

Alternatively, write about something you love—or something you hate. Either way, do it with feeling.

Do you know any Muslim girls who like square-dancing? Now I am not remotely a dancer, but I love t-shirts. In freshman gym class, I wasn't excited for the square dancing unit, but the best square dance team in class would win a t-shirt. At that point, I didn't care that the unit was about some dance based on old-fashioned rural and White European mountain-community barn dances, I just wanted that t-shirt and nothing would stop me from getting it. I was motivated to win, and I was determined to motivate my group to win.

The first few days I learned promenade and do-si-dos with students who were complete strangers to me. The unit wasn't a class favorite and most of the groups couldn't care less about square dancing. I became the leader of my group—students, some of whom probably looked at my skin and automatically thought I was a terrorist. With the incentive of winning this t-shirt, I told them my goal and got their support in achieving it.

Meanwhile, other groups would roll their eyes and just go through the motions; our team would skip and add a Texas Twirl at the end to give the dance a little more flare. We goofed off less at practice and added our own style to the dances. When it came to the singing parts, we all sang so loudly that our voices echoed throughout the school. Our energy and passion for square dancing followed us all day. When we saw each other in the hallway, we would do some quick dos-si-do before heading to class. Led by the Muslim girl who asked so many questions in class, our group actually enjoyed square dancing and our passion spread to other groups. Suddenly, there was serious competition as everyone tried to top us. I just told our group we just had to work even harder. In the semi-finals, our team didn't make a single mistake. Then came the finals and I encouraged our team to be even better.

We were flawless, so good that we would have qualified for the square-dancing Olympics if there was one. We Alabama-lefted our partners and though our palms were sweaty as we clapped, it was the best performance we had ever done. When it came to announce the winner, everyone knew it was us. That day I led my team to the square-dancing championship at my high school.

We won the shirts, and we wore them with pride. At that point, my goal was accomplished; I added another t-shirt to my collection. But this was just the beginning of my square-dancing journey. I realized this contest was bigger than some t-shirt that I wanted for my closet. I might not be able to put a square dancing championship on my resume but I could apply the hard work and passion I put into this goal into anything I do.

I learned from this that anything is possible and you should always strive to do more, even if you reach your goal. I also learned that if you can lead a group into supporting you and give your utmost, you will always succeed in some way. If I could do this with square dancing, I could do this with anything.

People see me as many things: the girl who works so hard to learn how to write a DBQ, the girl who fills her summer up with endless tasks such as summer courses and internships, the girl who stays up all night trying to understand bank curves in physics. What they don't see is that I am also what square dancing has made me—a professional square dancer. And I will continue to use the valuable skills I acquired in my classes and my life. I may even try to teach some of my Muslim friends to square dance—it's really fun!

This essay might have answered either of the first two prompts. It's a particularly compelling story with a great question for a lede. Who wouldn't want to read on after "Do you know any Muslim girls who like square dancing?" And she follows through with a story that is both interesting and informative about the writer. It's incidental that they happened to win the championship, but in this case, it makes for a better essay.

Rowing? Yes, rowing as in "*Row, row, row your boat, gently down the stream.*"

Every time I tell people from my neighborhood that I am a rower, I am forced to sing this song; most inner-city Hispanics have no idea what crew is or what an incredible sport it is! I grew up in Little Village, a predominantly Hispanic community in Chicago, part of a family of six. My parents, who only completed grammar school, emigrated from Mexico more than twenty years ago. They sought a better life, which included opportunities for their children to become educated. In my family we value education and hard work above everything else. I have watched my parents work tirelessly to ensure that my siblings and I get an education so we can avoid the hardships that they experienced. My parents have always told me that their greatest accomplishment is that all of their children work hard and appreciate the opportunities they have been given. My parents are the main reason I strive to excel in my education and why, for the past eight years, I have dedicated myself so completely and passionately to rowing.

I am part of a rowing training center, which provides underserved kids who would not be able to participate due to the cost, the opportunity to train for free. Rowing has taught me the most important lesson in life: there is no limit to what you can do as long as you have motivation and discipline, a lesson I have applied to my education. Years ago, people would tell me that I could not receive a good education because the schools in Little Village were low-performing academically. Yes, this is true, but that was no obstacle for me. It simply made me work harder. When the time came, instead of enrolling in my neighborhood high school, I applied to private high schools and for scholarships to help my parents pay for my tuition. My hard work was rewarded with a scholarship to St. James Academy.

Last year, my dad was unemployed and with tuition payments due it was hard for our family. However, I used my rowing experience to encourage my family to work together. Like rowers stroking together to move the boat, my family moved forward as a team. My mother found a part-time job, and my brothers and I helped with the chores at home while my father worked on finding a job. Ultimately, we were stronger than ever, and I am eternally grateful for this challenge because together we as a family worked harder than I ever thought we could and we succeeded. For me, it was a lot like having a rocky start in a race—everyone must work together to regain balance in the boat. If rowers cooperate to settle the boat and then pull extra hard, there is always a chance for a come-from-behind victory.

Rowing has also helped me put my education in perspective. I choose the most rigorous classes and challenge myself to work as hard as I can, which is why I take classes like AP Calculus and have a GPA above a 4.0. I think of it as training. My finish line will be to attend a prestigious college where I can earn a degree that will provide me with career opportunities. Attending St. James means waking up two hours earlier than I normally would to get ready for school and riding the bus for more than hour. But it also means new opportunities that I will take advantage of to make my parents, and the others who have supported me throughout my rowing and school career, proud. I know that hard work and determination in my studies, in rowing, and in every aspect of my life, will help me achieve any goal I set.

This is another essay that could have answered either of the first two prompts. In essence, it's a personal growth essay, Although the author lists her rowing accomplishments in her resume, and it is generally not desirable to duplicate your accomplishments in your essay, here it is not so much about how well she did but what rowing meant to her. You can't help but think she will do well in college, and if you have conveyed this in your essay, you have done a good job.

Chapter Six

The Supplemental Essay

So you've finished your Common App essay, and you think the worst is over. Maybe so, but in most cases, you're not done writing essays. You still have to contend with the supplemental essays that many schools require, usually one to three additional writing assignments. (Note that if you apply to ten schools that ask for an average of two supplemental essays, that means you have to write twenty essays plus your Common App essay. That's a lot of work.)

At one to five hundred words and generally shorter than the Common App essay, these supplemental essays are school-specific, although they tend to fall into common categories (see examples in this chapter). The supplemental essays are not as "make or break" as the Common App essay—a good supplemental essay is unlikely to gain you admission to your school, but a bad one may move you from the college's "Undecided" group to the "Rejected" group. That's why you must take them seriously.

Before we delve into the specifics of supplemental essays, you should know the same writing principles apply to these essays as to the Common App essay: Answer the question, stick to the word count, and be sure your grammar and spelling are correct (in shorter essays, mistakes stand out more). **But your most important goal in the supplemental essays is to tell the school more about yourself, things that may not be in your application or Common App essay. Many students view supplemental essays as a throwaway assignment; this is a mistake.**

Consider this a chance to give the reader a more complete profile of you.

Every school has its own supplemental essay questions, but many of the questions are variations on the same theme. In that respect, you can prepare essays for several schools, with the knowledge that you must tailor the details to the specific school. The most common supplemental essay question, and for some schools the only question, is a variant of why do you want to attend this school.

Why Do You Want to Attend (This School)?

The question asks why you want to attend this particular school, but implicit in this question is what you will bring to the school if you are admitted. So in the allotted word count, you must try to address both areas—why this school is a good fit for you and what makes you ideal for the school.

In terms of why you want to attend the school, the admissions reader is gauging your level of interest. This is where you want to demonstrate your knowledge about the school. If you have already visited the school, especially if you have done a tour and attended an information session, be sure to mention that. (Take notes on your tour and information session. You may be able to put some little-known facts in your essay.) You should talk about what you saw on your tour, who you talked to, and what impressed you about the campus and the student body. Did you talk to a professor or a current student? Explain how those interactions went. If you plan on visiting the school, say so—but do not lie about that. More likely than not, the school will check whether you visit.

Actual campus visits may not be practical or even available. In 2020–2021, most college visits were put on hold as a result of the COVID-19 pandemic. It's understood you may not have the time or be able to afford a visit, or you may live three thousand miles away. There are still ways you can and should show the reader that you are interested in the school. Many schools offer virtual tours and virtual information sessions; if a school you are thinking about offers a virtual tour, take it and describe it. Sign up for its virtual information session. In addition, you should follow the school on social media and visit its blog and website.

There are several things that may attract you to a school that you can include in your essay. The one that most students mention is academics—special courses or fields of study that the school features and that you may want to pursue.

Occasionally a school will offer research opportunities or study-abroad options that you think are particularly attractive. Sometimes a school features unique extracurricular activities that you want to become involved with. Again, these answers may involve some research on your part, but they can be helpful to your application because they demonstrate your interest.

One of the ways schools differentiate themselves is through campus life—traditions, social events, and campus activities. Some schools have a special sports pedigree. If you are a sports fan and follow that school, mention that. If you do, it's good to include a sentence using the school's nickname and colors (in that usage, if you refer to the school or team by its colors, capitalize the colors, for example, Maize and Blue for University of Michigan, Crimson Tide for the University of Alabama, Scarlet and Gray for The Ohio State University).

Remember, the purpose is to demonstrate your interest in the school. Many schools currently track levels of how much they are being followed digitally by prospective students, a trend that is likely to become more sophisticated in the future.

You can segue into talking about your personal pursuits, but *do not repeat information that can be found in your application or Common App essay.* For example, if you are interested in fashion design, and you have discussed that in your Common App essay or it is obvious from your activities list, talk about some other interest in this prompt. (You can mention fashion design if a prompt asks what you are considering majoring in.) Or you can talk about some other aspect of your life that is important to you. *You do not want the school to get the impression you are a one-dimensional person.* Is there something in your background or upbringing you haven't mentioned? This is a natural lead-in to the second part of the "why do you want to attend" prompt: What you will bring to the school if you are admitted.

Sell yourself. Tailor your response to the specific school. Are you from a rural environment applying to an urban school? Your experience will be valuable to the student body. By the same token, if you are from an inner-city background applying to a rural school, the same principle applies. Perhaps you have a special interest—musical, artistic, entrepreneurial—that dovetails with something the school specializes in (robotics? software development? interior decoration?). In your application, was there an extracurricular activity you were involved in that you didn't mention or mentioned only in passing? This prompt is where you can devote an entire paragraph to it. This is also where you can discuss some facet of your personality that separates you from other candidates and explain why you will be an asset to the school and its community.

Another common supplemental essay question regards community.

Describe How You Have Contributed to Your Community and How You Will Contribute to the Community at . . .

Again, this question is asking two things and you generally only have one to two hundred words to answer it. College is about more than just attending class, so it's a question about your extracurricular activities, that is, activities you haven't addressed elsewhere in your application. (Sometimes this prompt is alternatively worded in some form as "tell us about your extracurricular activities.") If you have an extracurricular that involves a charitable activity, describe it. Even if your extracurricular activity doesn't involve the larger community, schools understand that—everyone doesn't do charity work. However, if your extracurricular is only a personal thing, explain how it will help you engage with other students. Perhaps it's your religious affiliation. Are you a gamer? Explain how you will join that community at school.

This prompt is your chance for a little introspection—examine your interest and figure out how it will dovetail with the school you want to attend. This means learning about the culture of your school and perhaps a little about the student body. The reader will appreciate it if you show that, even in the limited format of two hundred words.

Sometimes this prompt is asked as "tell us about a community you belong to." You have the latitude to answer this in many ways—your ethnicity, your neighborhood, a specific interest, a sport you play, or a hobby. Feel free to tell the reader what community you are proud of. Keep in mind the purpose of the prompt: to learn more about you as an applicant and how you will fit in at their school.

SHORT ANSWER SUPPLEMENTAL QUESTIONS

Many schools want to get a fuller picture of you by asking a series of short answer questions: What is your favorite book, movie, song, and so on? Often, they just want the answer to the question; sometimes they want a short essay (e.g., Who is your hero and why?). Some guides advise you that there can be a trap in these questions, that is, the school is looking for a "wrong" answer. That may be true, but we advise you not to overthink your answers or dwell on them too long. There may be a wrong answer, but, in most cases, it would be hard to tell; so don't worry about it. Honesty is the best and most convenient approach. Your answers are unlikely to raise a flag in all but the most unusual situation. Use some common sense. Adolf Hitler would not be a good answer for your hero. It may not be advisable to give a hint to a religious school that you are an atheist, but, in general, be your authentic self. The reader is probably more interested in authenticity than in your actual answers. These are not the questions to spend a great deal of time on.

Here are some basic supplemental essay prompts and a couple of prompts from specific schools.

General Supplementals

Supplemental Prompt: **Please briefly elaborate on one of your extracurricular activities or work experiences. (Limit to 250 words.)**

> My friends and I wanted to rollerblade, not swim! However, when we arrived to blow off steam on a sunny June day in 2017, the Sandy Litwin Memorial Park (SLMP) in Deerlove, IL was flooded with mosquito-ridden, stagnant water. After research, I learned that SLMP's abundant supply of turfgrass caused the flooding. Unnatural to Illinois Plains, but inexpensive to plant, this shallow-rooted grass doesn't absorb excess water during high-rain periods.
>
> After my thwarted attempt to rollerblade through the SLMP, I contacted the local park district to create a 34,700 square foot rain garden, comprised of deep-rooted and native flowers, shrubs, and grasses designed to reduce flooding. Both low maintenance and beautiful, the rain garden appealed to officials, who agreed to support my proposal. Together, we removed large sections of the park's turfgrass and bought 1,000 plants and 220 pounds of seeds, spending the $5,687 in funds raised.

> I made posters and hosted seminars to recruit over thirty volunteers to plant my rain garden. Finally, on a wet Saturday morning in May 2018—nearly 11 months and over 200 hours of work later—a team of helpers joined me in building the garden.
>
> When I returned to the SLMP this past summer to rollerblade, the rain garden was serving its purpose. The park was dry and fully functional. What's more, the nearby Chicago River was exponentially cleaner without dirty stormwater flowing downstream. My hope is the rain garden will last for decades, permanently improving the local ecology.

Sometimes the essay writes itself; this is one of those times. There's nothing magic here—just a description of what the writer accomplished. But it's good in a subtle way. First of all, she explains in 250 words what was a fairly extensive project. That's not easy to do. Second, go back and look at the first sentence. It's a great lede. She used a couple of descriptive adjectives but didn't overuse them. Finally, an appropriate amount of detail; any more would have been too much, any less not enough. Full use of 250 words.

Prompt (Activities Essay): **If you could only do one of the activities you have listed in the Activities section of your Common Application, which one would you keep doing? Why? (Required for all applicants.) Limit to 150 words.**

> High Five Choir is a musical group for students of all abilities to sing and raise disability awareness. For forty minutes every day for the past three years, I've sung meaningful songs and created the best friendships I've ever known. Too often, we judge others without knowing them, or neglect to acknowledge their presence and purpose in our lives. There's something in the air of the choir room that puts these habits to rest. We're all differently abled: some use vocal chords to sing, others use sign language, and some express themselves through dance, while others use a smile. But it's through these differences that connections grow. What's more, those who are the most challenged in their abilities typically smile the biggest. High Five has given me lasting friendships, a refreshed perspective on life, and proof that goodness exists. I wish I could continue it for years to come.

Answers the prompt right away. Simple and from the heart. Exactly the type of essay you want to write. When you read it, you get a good picture of the writer, and she presents herself well. Warm and humble. It's so good, it would be great to see this essay expanded into her Common App essay. It's hard to sustain this approach for 650 words, but somehow you get the idea the author could pull it off.

Prompt: **Tell us how a book changed your life.**

> If I were to open a bookstore, the first book I would order would be "Seuss-isms: Wise and Witty Prescriptions for Living from the Good Doctor" by Dr. Seuss. As a child, I loved Seuss books for the colorful pages and crazy characters with names like Benjamin Bicklebaum and Fizza-ma-wizza-ma-dill. I appreciate Seuss books today as much as I did as a child, because I have found truths in them that have a great deal of significance. "Seuss-isms" is a compilation of life lessons, which embody a sense of how to live life positively, and with a sense of humor.
>
> Some of my favorite book quotes include, *"Don't cry because it's over. Smile because it happened.*" and "*Think and wonder, wonder and think.*" These were especially true for me in my fifth year at Camp Clearlake for Girls. On my last day, I could hardly contain my tears because every year it became more difficult to say goodbye to the place I called my second home and to the girls I referred to as my sisters.
>
> A sense of magic dwelled within Clearlake, like the magic that jumped off Dr. Seuss's pages. It was that rare place, where others could get to know the true me and where I was defined by my character and kindness, not by my accomplishments or talents. I cannot completely describe my experiences at Clearlake: sailing with the sunlight dancing in the waves and wind whispering through my hair, and the feelings of sisterhood and compassion shared by every girl despite significant differences in age, upbringing, life experiences and personality. Over five blissful summers, these experiences combined to create a canvas of memories. Each year after returning home, I was a little more confident, kind, and adventurous.
>
> My camp director encouraged me to live by Dr. Seuss's words, "*Don't cry because it's over. Smile because it happened.*" I knew then that I would never forget the beauty of the Northwoods, the call of the loon, and the song of my footfalls on Clearlake's graveled paths to self-discovery. I also realized this wasn't the end. By transforming me and all its daughters into young women with self-esteem and compassion, Clearlake gave me a gift I could bring anywhere. It shaped my love of nature and sense of adventure. I often reflect on the compassion of Clearlake's young women, and I work to replicate this spirit at home.

> During the last night of camp, everyone gathered around a campfire and sang, *"And although my journey has only begun, I can look back and see how far I've come."* This song defined Clearlake's gift to me—allowing me to grow, strive, achieve, look back on my progress, and continue to seek adventure.
>
> I was heartbroken when I had to leave, but I realize how lucky I was to experience this special place. All things must eventually come to an end but Dr. Seuss teaches us not to cry, but to smile and celebrate the glory of existence.

A nice, heartfelt, well-written essay. You learn about the author, and she comes off quite well. This is a good example of the author using the prompt to her best advantage.

Describe an academic or intellectual project, experience or pursuit of which you are particularly proud. (Limit to 75–150 words.)

> Everyone at my school must write a Junior Theme Research Paper with two guidelines: *it must be a topic about America, and a subject of profound interest to you.* I wrote about economic inequality in America. It made me question my beliefs and developed my critical thinking and writing skills. My research showed America has less economic mobility than other industrialized nations, which led me to conclude the American dream of economic success through hard work and merit is dwindling. Advancing now depends primarily on your family's affluence, education, and social connections. Globalization, a tilting of political life toward the interests of affluent individuals and corporations, and the failure of America's K–12 schools to produce enough skilled laborers to meet new technological demands were three main drivers of increasing income inequality. After months of research and multiple drafts, I was proud of my concise, persuasive, and passionate paper.

You have to choose your topics for your essays carefully. This is a good topic, but it is probably not the right topic for a 150-word maximum. It's a good essay, but it does not give the subject the attention it deserves in such a limited format. Ironically, this could have been the basis for a good Common App essay, and there is a "time when you challenged a belief" prompt. The topic would be better addressed in 650 words.

Supplemental Prompts by Schools

Illinois

Explain your interest in the major you selected and describe how you have recently explored or developed this interest, inside and/or outside the classroom. You may also explain how this major relates to your future career goals. Limit your response to 300–400 words. (Business Unassigned)

I have grown up with the goal of one day leading a business. Even when I was young, I always wanted to be a leader of everything I did, whether that was on a sports team, in a class group, or in church. Business leadership has become more important to me as I've aged, and while I still do not know what kind of business I want to lead, I know that it is a general goal for my life. The business unassigned major at the University of Illinois is a perfect way for me to start my career as a learner in the field of business. I admire the great business leaders today, such as Bill Gates and Warren Buffett, who believed in their own ideas and persevered to create lasting businesses. My sister graduated from the College of Business at Illinois, and I look up to her because of her experiences she has gained since then. She has told me that Illinois fosters students' knowledge about all things related to business their first two years, and then allows them to narrow into a passion for their major.

While my sister has been a role model for me, my interests in business have long been a part of my personality. During my sophomore year, I started converting my neighbor's old VCR's into DVD's. I was paid to do the tedious work, but it made me appreciate how business works. A simple favor grew, and I then was paid to convert my own family's VCR's. My other family friends heard of the work that I did, and I turned it into a little business. The work involved placing the VCR's into a machine that would automatically convert them to DVD's. It was very easy for a technologically savvy teenager, but it was time-consuming. I realized then that the more unique a business is, the greater chance it has to thrive. I named my business Media Conversion, a very complex name for a simple operation. It worked, however, and through networking, I made the most of my small business. At the University of Illinois, I hope to find a passion in the College of Business that can help me fine-tune my business skills so I can one day lead a large corporation, charity, or technology start-up, making huge improvements from my teenage business.

Again, another essay with an emphasis on leadership, this time in the field of business. (We advise staying away from "more unique" as used in the second paragraph. The sentence would read better as "I realized that a unique business has a greater chance to thrive.")

Tulane

Please describe why you are interested in attending Tulane University.

When I visited Tulane as I was starting my junior year, I didn't know what my dream school would look like. Moments after being on campus, I knew I had found it. Surrounded by a sea of greenery, I fell in love with Tulane as the tour unfolded. Walking past the mix of new and old architecture, I listened to my tour guide describe the great opportunities at the university. The school spirit was so evident that I immediately felt I belonged. This instant connection I made last year endures. I am confident that Tulane is the perfect choice for me. I haven't decided on a major, so I appreciate that Tulane does not require you to declare until fourth semester. I have a wide range of interests and enjoy the fact that at Tulane I can take classes in any undergraduate program. I am interested in French, psychology, and film studies, so being able to do a major or minor in all three is appealing.

The required first-year TIDES course is quite attractive. Tulane offers many interesting ways to fulfill this requirement, including classes on New Orleans Performance Culture, Visual Arts, and Making New Orleans. This program is a great aspect of the school because students can become better acquainted with the New Orleans community.

Attending a mid-size university is important to me, because I come from a high school of over 4,000 students. I want to attend a school with people from different backgrounds and meet as many people as possible. I also want to maintain personal relationships with my professors. Being a school of about 8,000 with an 8:1 student to faculty ratio, Tulane will allow me to get to know my professors.

Another great quality of Tulane is the commitment to the community. I admire that public service is a prerequisite for graduation. In high school, I played an active role in helping my community. I have worked with children at Lurie Children's Hospital, raised money for three different service groups, raised money to purchase Christmas gifts for a local family, and helped organize two blood drives. I have grown up giving back to the community and taking time to improve it. Tulane's service requirement aligns well with my values.

I want to study abroad and the program in Rabat, Morocco, is appealing. I have been to France to practice the language, but I have never traveled to Africa, so French-African culture is foreign to me. It would be an incredible experience to delve into the region's history and explore the nearby mountains and beaches. I appreciate that Tulane has a group of Peer Advisors who have studied abroad and will help prospective students prepare for their travels and assist with the application process.

Another attractive feature of Tulane is the French influence in New Orleans. I love the idea of being surrounded by French culture in the United States, which is something unique to New Orleans. I have always appreciated New Orleans' French traditions from the food, to the bustling activity in the French Quarter, to Mardi Gras. French culture and language have played a big role in my life, so it is important for me to have this continue in college. New Orleans is the perfect place to learn in depth about French culture.

I am also interested in the cultural arts in New Orleans, the home to many artists and dance companies. I have been dancing since I was little, and seeing live performances has always been a big part of my life. I believe dancers should support other dancers. Even though I do not wish to major in dance, I am grateful that Tulane offers dance classes to all students, regardless of major.

Because of the many opportunities that Tulane provides its students, from academics to culture, I am confident that Tulane is the perfect school for me and where I can develop, thrive, and reach my full potential. I am applying Early Decision, because I know I will be an involved member of the Tulane community and would be honored to call it my home.

There is nothing special about this essay, but it covers all the bases for this prompt. When you are called on to answer this type of prompt, these are the things you want to mention. The tour is especially important. You should always mention it when you have taken a tour of your prospective school. Colleges want to see your level of interest, and a tour is good evidence of interest.

Wake Forest

Have you visited the Wake Forest campus? If yes, tell us about your visit and with whom did you speak? (150 words or fewer)

After attending the Carolina Ballet Summer Intensive, I learned about Wake Forest University. I had one day between the end of the program and my flight home, so I decided to make the trip to the University.

Unfortunately, it was a Sunday during the summer, so I was not able to attend any formal presentations. Luckily, I did meet a Wake Forest student who was showing the school to her summer internship friends. I got to spend an hour touring the campus with her and learning about the school. Her enthusiasm for the school was electrifying and made me even more excited about the prospect of becoming a Wake Forest student. After spending time with her I began to see Wake Forest as the place where I could best channel my passions, including my love for dance and foreign language.

How did you become interested in Wake Forest University and why are you applying? (150 words or fewer)

Last summer, I attended the Carolina Ballet Summer Intensive and learned about the Wake Forest Dance Program. At first, I didn't consider the University because, in seeking a dance program, I only researched schools with a dance major. After hearing about Wake Forest's Dance Program, I researched the school. The more I learned, the more I could imagine four years learning and living among the Wake Forest's students and professors.

I believe the marriage between a superb liberal arts education and the strong dance program make Wake Forest an excellent fit for me. I am interested in the University's Business and Enterprise Management Major. If accepted, I would apply to study abroad through the Wake Forest University Barcelona: Business and Global Studies Program, given my strong love of the Spanish language. Wake Forest University is where I can pursue a strong liberal arts education, and become a better dancer.

Another important thing to talk about in your school essay is your interest and any special program at the school that dovetails with that interest.

Boston College

Boston College strives to provide an undergraduate learning experience emphasizing the liberal arts, quality teaching, personal formation, and engagement of critical issues. If you had the opportunity to create your own college course, what enduring question or contemporary problem would you address and why?

Economists claim it is one of the most sought-after traits in the 21st century workforce. Psychologists maintain it is mandatory for human connection. Neuroscientists assert it is hardwired into our brains. Sociologists warn that today's college students have less of it compared to college students a generation ago. St. Ignatius understood it is embodied in our call to serve others. What is it?

Empathy.

The college course I would create is one on becoming more humane: Empathy 101. Like many, I grew up hearing, "put yourself in someone else's shoes." As I reflect on my peers, and myself, I believe we are often empathetic. For instance, if one of my teammates has two tests tomorrow and our tennis match takes longer than expected, we all understand and share her "I'm going to be up all night studying" stress. Chances are we are quieter on the bus ride home so she can start studying.

As a generation that volunteers regularly, we have practice seeing and feeling things from others' perspectives. Yet sometimes millennials such as myself get caught up in our own issues. We are absorbed in how many Instagram "likes" we get and a bit too numb to pay attention to another news story of violence or a natural disaster. Unfortunately, sometimes the competition to succeed academically, in our extra-curricular and social activities, is so overwhelming that we get lost in an "every man for himself" mentality.

But my family values and Jesuit education taught me we should be there for each other, and that begins with empathy. Empathy is more than just a nicety. It is the cornerstone of human connection, and thus is crucial to the well-being of individuals and society. Studies indicate empathy can reduce depression, increase self-esteem, and boost the immune system. It increases employee productivity, decreases student drop-out rates, and reduces divorce. Empathy is touted as a way to confront social injustice and is the most valuable resource in conflict resolution.

Clearly empathy can be transformative, and I believe it can transform my generation from the "me" generation to the "us" generation where everyone in the human family sticks together. Fortunately, we can improve on our innate ability and learn to be more empathetic. Next year I hope to become part of the Boston College Community, a community of men and women for others, a community I'm confident would eagerly register for Empathy 101.

Whenever possible, a good school essay should reflect the values of the school. In this case, the author has done a fine job of reflecting the values of the school. In turn, that reflects well on the author. In the fourth paragraph "such as myself" should read "such as me." Writers often resort to the reflexive "myself" when "me" is correct.

Chapter Seven

Special Creative Questions

This is a trend that more schools are using outside of the traditional application to learn more about their applicants. You are given your choice of several unusual questions and you must use your creativity to answer them. Some schools may even allow you to answer a question you devised. The University of Chicago was a pioneer in this approach, and they offer different questions every year. Most of these prompts have been submitted by University of Chicago students. From the University of Chicago website, here are some of their classic creative prompts from the past.

> Due to a series of clerical errors, there is exactly one typo (an extra letter, a removed letter, or an altered letter) in the name of every department at the University of Chicago. Oops! Describe your new intended major. Why are you interested in it and what courses or areas of focus within it might you want to explore? Potential options include Commuter Science, Bromance Languages and Literatures, Fundamentals: Issues and Texts, Ant History . . . a full list of unmodified majors ready for your editor's eye is available here.
>
> —Inspired by Josh Kaufman, AB'18

> Joan of Arkansas. Queen Elizabeth Cady Stanton. Babe Ruth Bader Ginsburg. Mash up a historical figure with a new time period, environment, location, or occupation, and tell us their story.
>
> —Inspired by Drew Donaldson, AB'16

Alice falls down the rabbit hole. Milo drives through the tollbooth. Dorothy is swept up in the tornado. Neo takes the red pill. Don't tell us about another world you've imagined, heard about, or created. Rather, tell us about its portal. Sure, some people think of the University of Chicago as a portal to their future, but please choose another portal to write about.

—Inspired by Raphael Hallerman, Class of 2020

What's so odd about odd numbers?

—Inspired by Mario Rosasco, AB'09

Little pigs, French hens, a family of bears. Blind mice, musketeers, the Fates. Parts of an atom, laws of thought, a guideline for composition. Omne trium perfectum? Create your own group of threes, and describe why and how they fit together.

—Inspired by Zilin Cui, Class of 2018

How are apples and oranges supposed to be compared? Possible answers involve, but are not limited to, statistics, chemistry, physics, linguistics, and philosophy.

—Inspired by Florence Chan, AB'15

Heisenberg claims that you cannot know both the position and momentum of an electron with total certainty. Choose two other concepts that cannot be known simultaneously and discuss the implications. (Do not consider yourself limited to the field of physics.)

—Inspired by Doran Bennett, AB'07

Susan Sontag, AB'51, wrote that "[s]ilence remains, inescapably, a form of speech." Write about an issue or a situation when you remained silent, and explain how silence may speak in ways that you did or did not intend. *The Aesthetics of Silence*, 1967.

—Anonymous Suggestion

So where is Waldo, really?

—Inspired by Robin Ye, AB'16

Find x.

—Inspired by Benjamin Nuzzo, an admitted student from Eton College, UK

Dog and Cat. Coffee and Tea. Great Gatsby and Catcher in the Rye. Everyone knows there are two types of people in the world. What are they?

—Inspired by an anonymous alumna, AB'06

How did you get caught? (Or not caught, as the case may be.)

—Inspired by Kelly Kennedy, AB'10

Chicago author Nelson Algren said, "A writer does well if in his whole life he can tell the story of one street." Chicagoans, but not just Chicagoans, have always found something instructive, and pleasing, and profound in the stories of their block, of Main Street, of Highway 61, of a farm lane, of the Celestial Highway. Tell us the story of a street, path, road—real or imagined or metaphorical.

—Anonymous Suggestion

"Don't play what's there, play what's not there."—Miles Davis (1926–1991)

—Inspired by Jack Reeves

The essays you create from these prompts are not a direct reflection of your personality. But schools use them to get an idea of your creativity, writing ability, and ingenuity. Sometimes you can research a subject and use some facts to enhance your essay. Done well, this can impress a reader. These essays are personal; no one can tell you how to write them. For that reason, you should give them some thought and use your imagination. This is an opportunity, perhaps your best opportunity, to take chances with your application. There are obviously no wrong answers to these prompts but some essays are better than others, and the best essays are often the weirdest.

Perhaps the best advice we can give you about questions like these is to show you some examples of successful creative essays. After you read these, you may get ideas on how to approach these prompts. Without question, the most important takeaway is that you want to make your creative essay readable and entertaining. You'll want someone to read your Common App essay and your supplementals to give you feedback. This is the one essay you may want more than one person to read, not so much for feedback but to see if they enjoyed reading it.

The following are some UChicago prompts and creative essays.

What does Play-Doh™ have to do with Plato?

What does Play-Doh have to do with Pluto? First off, this prompt is unclear. Does it mean compare Play-Doh with Pluto the "planet," or Pluto the dog? Well, since the prompt is ambiguous, I will discuss both Plutos and what they have to do with Play-Doh.

The key issue here is respect—I've got a bone to pick (and it's not the one that belongs to Pluto the dog). Essentially, even though they are all about the same age, Play-Doh gets all the respect while the two Plutos get absolutely none. ZERO. Personally, I'm angry because I don't think that's fair. The two Plutos deserve just as much, if not more, respect than Play-Doh.

Admittedly, Play-Doh was a clever invention. But it was invented in the 1930's as a wallpaper cleaner. A wallpaper cleaner? Big deal. I'm sure back in the 1930's, nobody gave much respect to this wallpaper cleaner, which is basically quick-drying clay. Then Play-Doh got lucky. It caught on as a fun, moldable craft. All those Baby Boomer kids got bored with their Hula-Hoops and their Etch-a-Sketches, so pretty soon every Jane and Jimmie was playing with it. It didn't hurt that it also caught on with kindergarten teachers. Plus it had a hokey logo—the little boy in a blue beret. So by 1998, Play-Doh, the former wallpaper cleaner, got inducted into the National Toy Hall of Fame in New York. Now that's respect.

Meanwhile in 1930, about the same time the wallpaper cleaner was being invented, Illinois native Clyde W. Tombaugh discovered a new planet. Imagine that, there are only eight planets and Clyde discovers the ninth, Pluto. That should get some respect. But then what happens? Because Pluto is smaller than the other planets and is farther away from Earth, it gets demoted to a "dwarf planet" in 2006. What is a dwarf planet anyway? Just because it still has the word "planet" in its name doesn't ease the pain from its demotion. So what if it hangs out in the Kuiper Belt? Can't it still be a planet? Play-Doh gets in the Hall of Fame and Pluto gets kicked out of the planet club. It's a good thing Clyde Tombaugh didn't live to hear the appalling news of Pluto's demotion. That sound you hear is Clyde spinning in his grave. No respect for Pluto, "the dwarf."

And then there's Pluto the dog. Another example of no respect. Pluto gets into a Disney cartoon in 1930 when people are figuring out how to clean their wallpaper and Clyde Tombaugh is busy at his telescope. Pluto does well in his small roles and in 1934 he gets his own cartoon and gives a great performance. Does he become a star? Not on your life. He's not even the top dog at Disney. Ask people to name a Disney dog and you will get Goofy every time. Sure, Pluto has a good reputation, but no respect. Compare him to the big stars, Mickey and Donald. I bet you can name both Mickey and Donald's girlfriends, but what Pluto's girlfriend's name? See what I mean? (Her name is Dinah the Dachshund, in case you were wondering.) Every other animal Walt Disney created in the 1930's got dialogue. Pluto just chased cars. No respect.

Play-Doh is just a clump of flour, water, and salt. Yet it gets celebrated by millions of people around the world. What do Pluto, the dwarf planet, and Pluto, the dog, get? The short end of the stick. They didn't do anything to deserve this mistreatment. Give Pluto a chance—and some respect, for Clyde Tombaugh and Walt Disney's sake.

On top of this, the two Plutos get confused with each other. You are never sure which one people are referring to. What does Play-Doh get confused with? A great Greek classical philosopher. . . . **WAIT A MINUTE. WHOOPS, I JUST REREAD THE PROMPT. IT SAID PLATO, NOT PLUTO**! I'm sorry. It's too late to change my essay. Never mind. . . .

Admit it, you wouldn't believe if someone told you that you could misread the prompt and still write a successful essay; not only a successful essay, but one about misreading the prompt. This author took a chance, but it paid off (this student was accepted to the University of Chicago). This is the purpose of the creative question—to encourage you to take chances with your imagination and your writing.

If you look past the risk-taking aspect, you will see that it contains all the elements of a strong essay. There is a premise: comparing Pluto the dog and Pluto the planet (Play-Doh really has nothing to do with the essay). The author has done research—on the planet, on the Disney character, even on Pluto the dog's girlfriend. And it has a payoff: misreading the essay. There is even a little humor in the conclusion. The shock value is in the "misreading of the prompt," which the author obviously didn't misread, but its most important function is to serve as a good payoff. This creative essay demonstrates it helps to develop a good premise and supplement it with a strong payoff.

Joan of Arkansas. Queen Elizabeth Cady Stanton. Babe Ruth Bader Ginsburg. Mash up a historical figure with a new time period, environment, location, or occupation, and tell us their story.

A Modern-Day Biblical Tale of a Righteous Man

In Genesis, a righteous man named Noah took his family, along with a male and female pair of every animal, and saved them from The Flood by herding them on an ark for forty days and forty nights. When the Flood receded, he released his children and the animals to repopulate the Earth.

Few people know about his great-great-great-great-great-great-great-great-great grandson, Joakim, a righteous man who did something nearly as heroic. Like his ancestor, Joakim Noah was tall and muscular, a basketball player with plenty of hair on his face. One day—perhaps it was in his genes—he realized that the leather skins of animals were used to make basketballs. Out of kindness, again—perhaps it was in his genes—he took on the mission to stop this at all costs and save the animals. In the dead of night, he snuck into leather factories across the Earth, where the animals were warehoused. Like his famous ancestor, he saved the animals by collecting them on an ark. The animals of the second Noah's Ark sensed the imminent danger of the factories and were anxious to escape.

After returning the animals to their rightful birthplaces, he decided to return to his rightful birthplace. He left his home in Chicago to go back to New York to play for the Knicks. Unfortunately for him, his mission caused unintended problems. The next morning, when the factory workers returned to their warehouses, they realized that their animals were missing, so they had no choice but to take a break from producing leather. With the production of leather halted, the number of basketballs soon dried up. Because of this, the Knicks found themselves practicing with too few balls. And because their practices were in vain, they began to perform poorly in games.

Because the Bible says confession is good for the soul, Noah did the honorable thing and disclosed that he was to blame. Initially, General Manager Jackson from Chicago, and the other players, wanted to kick him off the team. However, Noah called them together and explained that the righteous thing was to play with rubber balls and balls made of synthetic materials.

Like his ancestor rescuing the animals from The Flood, Joakim showed his compassion for animals by sacrificing leather basketballs. The Lord rewarded the Knicks for Noah's righteousness by granting them the NBA Championship.

The moral is that for Noah II, getting the animals on the Ark was a long, tiring process, but he, too, was rewarded by The Lord. Using the

> skills he learned on the basketball court, he was careful to shepherd others. And just as with his ancestor, his family prospered as well. His mother, Cecilia Rodhé, inspired by her son's actions and compassion for others, joined forces with him to create Noah's Ark Foundation, which fosters an alternative path for animals destined to be slaughtered. This foundation monitors and improves the emotional and physical well-being of animals. The foundation that Noah and his mother created thrives as a testimony to their righteousness. The Lord works in mysterious ways.

This essay illustrates how you can go in almost any direction, but even if you have an interesting premise, you have to be able to follow through on it. Here, it's pretty easy to think of a historical mashup, all it takes is a play on someone's name. But creating a payoff can be difficult. We have seen a number of students think of a brilliant premise, and then struggle to find a payoff. In this case, the premise is good—a mashup of Biblical Noah with a modern-day basketball player—but the idea does not work unless there is a payoff. That's why Noah's Ark Foundation is what makes the essay. And the beauty of it is that Joakim Noah really did create a foundation for animals with his mother. The writer found the payoff by doing some research. With a premise and payoff, all the writer has to do is fill in the blanks with some well-written creative sentences about basketballs. The lesson is that sometimes a little research can solve your problem by finding a payoff for your premise and making for an enjoyable essay as well.

Were pH an expression of personality, what would be your pH and why? (Feel free to respond acidly! Do not be neutral, for that is base!)

> "Do I contradict myself? Very well then, I contradict myself, I am large, I contain multitudes"
>
> —Walt Whitman, *Leaves of Grass*

> When an acid and base mix together, they neutralize each other to create water, and are assigned the pH of 7. Water is two hydrogen atoms bonded to an oxygen atom, precisely as the laws of chemistry predict. Yet water glistens with magic unpredictability in Monet's "Water Lilies" and forms the droplets I watch race down the window of our family minivan. Water ebbs and flows, freezes and evaporates—scientific and poetic in equal measure. The number 7 seems to fall short in its description of water.

Water cannot be described by a single number, and neither can I. If I were to average every experience over my 18 years, every moment of wonder and facet of my personality, the result would not truly convey who I am. In water, hydrogen and hydroxide ions exist in equilibrium, reacting and ionizing without pause. Similarly, I am nuanced, contradictory, and more complex than a number.

People love to create order from chaos. We yearn to draw lines, categorize, and attach numbers and labels. Our greatest failing is in trying to apply this logic to individuals. A person cannot be summarized merely as a series of test scores, a salary, or an IQ. When we describe a person using numbers, as we might describe a solution's pH, we lose crucial aspects of what it means to be human.

Walt Whitman tells me that I am large and that I contain multitudes, so I say that I cannot be described by mere numbers. For each triumph, misstep, discovery, and for each bland and beautiful moment in between, I am a new version of myself. My personality, who I am now, and how I fit into the world, is more than an average, or a test score. It is the sum of every self I've ever been, and every self I'll ever be. How could anyone assign that a number?

This is a wonderful essay. It's not long, 338 words, but read it over and see how many different things the author incorporates: chemistry, a quote by Walt Whitman, a painting by Monet. And at the same time, she affords the reader a glimpse of her personality. It's an excellent example of how a good essay does not have to be long. In fact, the best essays are often short. Each of the four paragraphs is self-contained, you could write an effective essay with any one of them. And the transitions are smooth. It's also a good illustration of how to use a quote in your essay. The quote is not what you would expect with a prompt about acid-base chemistry. Notice how she introduces the essay with the quote and then circles back to it in the conclusion. The last line, a question, makes for a compelling ending.

Alice falls down the rabbit hole. Milo drives through the tollbooth. Dorothy is swept up in the tornado. Neo takes the red pill. Don't tell us about another world you've imagined, heard about, or created. Rather, tell us about its portal. Sure, some people think of the University of Chicago as a portal to their future, but please choose another portal to write about.

In the third corner of the world, past mountains, oceans, rivers, and hills, sits a forest—a forest so deep and long that no man has ever made it through and come back to tell the tale. Foggy, lovely, lush, and deep, the density of the forest creates very little light, permitting only a few feet of visibility at a time. Only the squeaking of unseen birds breaks the constant buzz of cicadas heard from miles around this forest.

There is only one known path which offers entrance into these deep woods: a twisted and knotty trail for the width of about one man. The path is meant to be taken alone.

Along the path of the forest, the earth routinely quakes every few hours, sending spiders the size of men into a howling frenzy. Purple polka dotted mushrooms grow out of larger scarlet striped mushrooms, which grow out of taupe trees. Despite the natural darkness of the forest, creatures who have developed varying degrees of bioluminescence illuminate the trail.

Finally, after miles upon miles of darkness, the path enters a small clearing. Short grass and daisies dot the area around a lake. If the lake were a conservative field, the flux of the wave magnitude would be low, but the curl would be high. The water is quiet, but the muggy blue holds secrets older than the abiotic fairies. Algae and duckweed dot the surface; scaly fish and other predatory creatures break the surface of the water with their dorsal fins. Despite the darkness, the inky liquid is intensely alive.

The waters are continuously swirling, shifting, shaking, around a small island at the base of the saddle of the hyperbolic paraboloid of flitting fairies. Golden, sparkling bulbs flit up and down in the moonlight darkness, in this forest, their brightness pulsing like a heartbeat or metronome. Every once in a while, one of the bulbs will glimmer a soft pink or blue, or perhaps a light beige. Under the taxonomic classification of abiotic fairies, these small creatures are fierce guardians. Out there, spiraling in hyperbolic paraboloid patterns over a murky lake, they look as numerous as stars in the Milky Way.

In order to reach the island, diamond encrusted granite and quartz stepping-stones dot a short path across the murky water. However, traversing these wet and thinly covered mossy stones is a challenge. The surface of these stones is impossible to see after decades of accumulated filth. At the top of the slipperiness of the rocks, the occasional animal fin—whether fish, mammal, or reptilian—slicing the water next to these stones is enough to distract a person to fall in. Absolute concentration must be utilized to shimmy across the ragged boundary.

A wanderer may manage to make it into the hollow of the forest, across the water and onto the island, but the journey still isn't over. These fairy guardians are hot to the touch, but with their extraordinarily high velocity, avoiding skin contact is almost impossible; they charge in swarms at

> an intruder. It's rumored in nearby villages that when lightning strikes in the center of the forest, a man has died at the hands of the electric fairies.
>
> But if a man can sneak into the center of the paraboloid, he'll find a crystal fountain, engraved with runic markings, bubbling with a green chunky juice slugging out of a brown pipe. Drinking this liquid is said to lead to a mysterious portal. It is not a physically transportive portal, but rather a mental one. Drinking from this fountain permits transcendence of the human condition. With this information, there is no suffering, only unconditional understanding—this sludge reveals the meaning of life, love, fear, and anger. He who drinks it will understand the meaning and purpose of life. Everything leading to this point of transcendence will become completely clear.
>
> That is, if he can also survive the journey out of the forest.

It's an off-beat prompt and an off-beat essay. The beauty of the open-ended prompts of the University of Chicago is that they grant the writer a degree of freedom to employ creativity. It is hard to imagine being able to write this type of free-form essay for the standard Common App prompts. But how else would the reader learn about this facet of the student's personality? And while this is not your standard college essay, it has all the elements of a good one. And it has a great ending. Powerful and unexpected. More schools should consider adopting that open-ended format. It brings out the best in some students.

Some essays from creative questions from other schools follow.

Dartmouth

***Oh, The Places You'll Go* is one of the most popular books by "Dr. Seuss" (Theodore Seuss Geisel, Dartmouth Class of 1925). Where do you hope to go? What aspects of Dartmouth's curriculum or community might help you get there? (100 max)**

> I hope to be a successful leader of a business while also living a balanced life with a loving and active lifestyle. These are broad goals, but the different aspects of Dartmouth's tight-knit community will help me achieve them. The liberal arts curriculum of Dartmouth is key since it allows for self-exploration and will help me find a true passion. Dartmouth also promotes service and leadership through its fraternities, while also encouraging athletic participation and focusing on nature, all of which I hold keen interest in. Overall, Dartmouth's emphasis on being well-rounded fits my personality and habits perfectly.

"Won't you be my neighbor?" was the signature catchphrase of Fred Rogers, the creator and host of *Mister Rogers Neighborhood.* What kind of neighbor will you be in our undergraduate community at Dartmouth? What impact have you had on the neighbors in your life? (250–300)

> At Dartmouth, I would be a very engaged and friendly neighbor not just to my fellow classmates, but also to my professors, the town of Hanover, and the overall Dartmouth community. The best neighbors always say hello, do nice things without being asked, and are always there when you need them. This is obviously most important for my roommate, who I will always respect and help out. In the learning neighborhood, participation in class is essential. For me, participation in the community is how I would make my presence known. At Dartmouth, I hope to be a constant participant in different leadership groups because I love getting involved in diverse opportunities. I also hope to participate in many recreational activities and keep myself healthy, in addition to taking advantage of the unique opportunities that the Dartmouth Outing Club provides in the beautiful surrounding areas.
>
> So far in my life, I have always tried my hardest to be a good neighbor to all people. I take pride in being a leader of different groups of people around me, and I feel that this is one of the greatest parts of my identity. Being a leader is something that comes naturally to me, and part of my leadership skill is that I always try to be inclusive. For example, in the lunchroom, if someone doesn't have a group to sit with, I always take charge and tell them to come sit with my friends and me. Besides being inclusive, I think one of the reasons I am a great neighbor is my overall personality. I try and greet everyone, whether I've known them for years or seconds. Trying to be this warm presence and making others feel comfortable is why I would be a good neighbor at Dartmouth.

There is nothing extraordinary about these essays except for the fact they emphasize the type of values schools are looking for. Leadership is a particularly important value. (Unfortunately, not everyone can be a leader. Don't make it up.) But if you happen to be a leader in any facet of your life, make sure you emphasize that. It will be an attractive addition to your application, especially if your recommendation letter from a coach, teacher, or work supervisor mentions it. Being a good neighbor or part of a community is another important characteristic to schools. They want to know if you will be a fit in their particular community.

Virginia

What work of art, music, science, mathematics, or literature has surprised, unsettled, or challenged you, and in what way? (250ish)

While I am not a musician, I have always been obsessed with many different genres of music. I listen to music when I am doing homework, during workouts, in the car, and when I am relaxing. One of my all-time favorite songs, and one that made me think about many different issues in the world, is "Where is the Love?" by the Black Eyed Peas. The first lyrics of the song are, "What's wrong with the world, mama?" The song goes on to name all the different issues plaguing the country, and the looming question is in the title of the song. While it is a very catchy song and was instantly popular in the United States, it says many unfortunate truths about the state of the country. It was released in 2003, when I was only 5 years old. However, as I have gotten older, while the music is just as great, I have realized that the song's message is essential for our country moving forward.

The issues discussed in the song are still problems over a decade letter. As a person who values peace and diplomacy, I wish that terrorism, wars, crime, and other examples of violence would stop all over the world. I realize this is an impossibility, but I took "Where is the Love?" to be a personal challenge. While I can't control countries or make decisions that will end poverty or other problems, I can be a confident voice in my own community. I can value my family and friends, and I can use words to settle differences with people who disagree with me. And the most important takeaway for me from this song was very subtle. If I can spread love around me, it will only grow. Hopefully one day the world will get this message.

Remember, be positive.

Student self-governance, which encourages student investment and initiative, is a hallmark of the U.Va. culture. In her fourth year at U.Va., Laura Nelson was inspired to create Flash Seminars, one-time classes that facilitate high-energy discussion about thought-provoking topics outside of traditional coursework. If you created a Flash Seminar, what idea would you explore and why?

If I created a Flash Seminar, I would call it "The Art of Politics," and it would feature discussion about how different songs, movies, television shows, paintings, and other forms of art and entertainment make political statements. It would also explore how art and entertainment, as well as the media as a whole, have a tremendous influence on politics. Different artists often have political alliances and hope to make political statements, and I believe that a Flash Seminar in this area would bring many opinions and ideas together. This would be successful because many students at the University of Virginia have some form of political ideology, and all students have some fundamental ideas and values that they hold true. I also know that most students have some passion in the arts, whether that is in some type of movie genre, a music genre, or an art medium.

Through these diverse interests, which form infinite combinations of political ideals and artistic feelings, people who participate in my Flash Seminar could discuss their own feelings while also critiquing and praising different works of art for the political ideas they present. While some works of art could be as humorous as Seth Rogen's North Korean parody "The Interview," and some could be as gravely serious as Florence Owens Thompson's "Migrant Woman" photograph from the Great Depression, they could all be discussed with intelligence and the wide-ranging opinions of the student body.

When you venture into politics, a sensitive subject, make sure you seek to promote a constructive dialogue.

We are looking for passionate students to join our diverse community of scholars, researchers, and artists. Answer this question, which corresponds to the school/program you selected above, in a half page or roughly 250 words. College of Arts and Sciences—What work of art, music, science, mathematics, or literature has surprised, unsettled, or challenged you, and in what way?

Every day, thousands of people listen to the United Airlines theme song, and most of them don't realize that they are listening to one of the iconic songs of the twentieth century. The theme, George Gershwin's "Rhapsody in Blue," is not merely some trivial commercialized gimmick; it is a legendary masterpiece that changed the way I play and experience music.

I discovered the song in the book American Standards while rummaging through the compartment of my family's old piano bench. The first time I heard the song I broke out in goosebumps. The complexity, the smoothness, the grandeur, and the unexpected turns of the piece elicited the most powerful emotions in me. I knew I had to learn this song.

During the next seven months, "Rhapsody in Blue" became my greatest enemy, my best friend, and my confidant all at once. To hear a masterfully crafted song is one thing, but to learn to play it on the piano is to enter into a dialogue with the composer, speaking to each other through different eras. Gershwin captivated me, and on some level, I felt as if I had entered his mind. At times, my intimacy with the piece even scared me. I found myself frustrated when others disliked the song or thought of it only as a commercial for United Airlines. I accepted the challenge of changing people's perception of the song, encouraging my friends and family to listen while I explained the song's majesty.

On a warm May afternoon, I finally memorized the piece. I was the only one in the room, but I'd like to think Mr. Gershwin was listening. I hope he was proud.

This is a nice essay. The author communicates his love for the Gershwin classic, but, at the same time, he communicates a lot about his personality. He is exactly what they are looking for according to the prompt: a passionate student.

Chapter Eight

Special Usage Rules for College Essays

When you are writing your college essays, you will employ a number of terms and usages that don't appear commonly in other types of writing. These are all questions we have encountered in college essays. Now a usage error will not earn you a rejection, obviously, but it never hurts to be familiar with the correct way to refer to these terms. It shows attention to detail, and that is one of the things schools are looking for in their candidates.

There is more than one way to write many of the terms listed here, so in certain cases there is no absolute answer, and, in fact, some of these usages are in flux. If you are referring to a specific school, you should check the school website to see what the school prefers (e.g., first reference—University of Michigan's Ross School of Business, second reference—Michigan Ross).

Here is a general guide that you can refer to. It generally adheres to *The Associated Press Stylebook 2020–2022* and *Merriam-Webster's Collegiate Dictionary 11th Edition*. This list is obviously not all-inclusive and if you have any questions, as always, when in doubt look it up.

Academic Degrees: Capitalize a degree that is part of a title but do not use periods: *BS, MD, JD, PhD*. Some style guides suggest using a period; make sure either way you are consistent. When referring to a degree in general terms use lowercase and the possessive apostrophe (it is not master or masters). *I want to obtain a master's degree. I am currently working on my bachelor's degree.* If you are referring to a specific degree, capitalize and do not use an apostrophe: John Smith, Master of Fine Arts. Patricia Jones, Bachelor of Sciences.

Academic Year: The first time you use the academic year, use lowercase for the season and the full year, no comma: *fall term 2021.* After that, you can abbreviate the year with a backward apostrophe (on a Mac: Option + Shift +]; in Word: Ctrl + Q, Quote, Quote): *fall term '21.*

Adviser vs. Advisor: Adviser has always been the preferred traditional usage, but advisor has gained in popularity.

Alumnus: A man who has attended a school is an *alumnus*. A woman who has attended a school is an *alumna.* More than one man or a group of men and women are *alumni.* A group consisting exclusively of women are *alumnae.*

Capitalize: The following should all be capitalized: names of apps (e.g., YouTube, Zoom), blogs, books, comic strips or cartoons, films, journals, magazines, newspapers, operas, paintings, plays, poems, radio and television programs, record albums, songs, video games, websites.

Class Year: Capitalize the word Class when referring to a specific graduation class. *My mother was part of the Class of 1989.* If you want to refer to a class and abbreviate to two digits, use a backward apostrophe: *Patricia Jones '89*. Freshman, sophomore, junior, and senior are not capitalized when referring to class year designations.

Colors: Although colors are not capitalized in general usage, capitalize when you are referring to the colors of a specific school. *The LSU Purple and Gold. The University of North Carolina colors are Carolina Blue and White.*

Days/Dates: Days should always be capitalized (and written out completely in all but informal communication). *Friday is my favorite day of the week*. Months should always be capitalized but can be abbreviated when referring to a specific date—remember to use a period at the end of the month abbreviation (*Nov. 22, 1963*).

Dogs: Some students write essays about their pets. Rules vary; some guides advise capitalizing the breed. Most rules suggest the only words that should be capitalized are words that come from proper nouns: *Yorkshire terrier, basset hound, poodle.*

Earth: Earth is a common topic in college essays. Capitalize Earth when referring to it as a planet or in terms of astronomy. *The Earth* *is larger than Mars.* Do not capitalize earth if you are referring to the soil or in a general sense. *I want to study earth sciences.* The same rule applies to the sun and the moon. *The Earth is smaller than the Sun but larger than the Moon. Saturn has many moons.*

Email/E-mail: Email was once the traditional spelling but e-mail is the preferred usage today. Either usage is correct, but again consistency is the most important thing.

Ethnicity: The current rule for African American, Asian American, Native American is that no hyphen is necessary. Black and white are acceptable as adjectives. *Black teachers, white students.* Current usage is that Black is always capitalized, but white is not. The terms Blacks and whites are generally not used by themselves as plurals to describe populations or groups of people anymore. There is no clear consensus on Hispanic/Latino/Latina/LatinX. If a school you are applying to has a guide that mentions which term it prefers, use that one. If not, use the term you are comfortable with and be consistent.

Facebook: Social media companies like Facebook and Instagram are capitalized.

Google: Current style is to capitalize Google, when it is used as a noun. It is also becoming common to capitalize when it is used as a verb. *I Googled the information for my paper.* However several guides still suggest using lowercase if using as a verb, in the manner of Xerox, which is generally lowercase as a verb. *I xeroxed several copies of my paper.*

GPA: If you are referring to your GPA, it should be capitalized (*My GPA is 3.95*).

Grades: Grades are capitalized. *I received an A last semester.* When discussing plural grades do not use apostrophes. *I have two As and four Bs on my transcript.*

Health Care: If you are referring to the delivery of health services, that is, health care as a noun, split the words. *Health care is becoming more expensive every year.* If you are using the term as an adjective, make it one word: *healthcare costs, healthcare personnel.*

High School: It's high school, two words. Never highschool. This is among the most common errors in college essays. Two words.

Internet: In Great Britain, internet is usually lowercase. In the United States, most style guides have switched to this style; do not capitalize internet.

Italics: Italicize book titles, newspapers (but not the word *the*—The *New York Times*), journals, magazines, plays, long poems (long enough to appear in a book by themselves), films, radio and television programs, artworks, names of ships and aircraft (*Apollo 11*). Italicize short phrases you really want to emphasize. Italicize unfamiliar foreign words the first time you use them. There is no general rule for certain terms (*E. coli*) and in those cases, consistency rules the day.

Judaism, Islam, Christianity: All religions should be capitalized. God should be capitalized when referring to the Supreme Being worshipped by the major religions. It should not be capitalized when it is used in another sense—*Elvis was a rock-and-roll god.* Capitalize but do not use italics or quotation marks for the Bible and the Qur'an. Do not use italics or quotation marks when you are mentioning individual books and suras (when named and not numbered): *John 3:16 is a well-known passage of the Bible.* Specific editions of the Bible are italicized: *New International Version, King James Bible.* The chief religious figure of a synagogue is a rabbi. As a general term, it is not capitalized—*I spoke with the rabbi.* As a title followed by an identified person, it is capitalized—*I spoke with Rabbi Cohen.*

Majors: If you are referring to your major, it should not be capitalized (*I want to major in chemistry*). The exception to the rule on majors is languages (*I want to major in French*). Likewise, do not capitalize the names of classes you took in grade school or high school, unless it was a language (*I took math, science, social studies, and English*). Capitalize (and use quotations for) the name of a specific class (I took "*Poetry in the Middle Ages*"). Capitalize AP (advanced placement) and IB (International Baccalaureate) when referring to these specialized classes.

Military: Capitalize the branches of the US military—Army, Navy, Air Force, Marines. Other countries military branches are usually not capitalized—Russian army, Japanese navy.

Nonprofit: Nonprofit is a noun and it is not hyphenated. Non-profit is incorrect. Not-for-profit is a similar term that can be a noun or an adjective. *I intend to work for a not-for-profit organization this summer.* Not-for-profit is hyphenated.

Numbers: Numbers less than 10 should be spelled out. Numbers greater than 10 can either be spelled out or written as numerals. The only exception is a sentence that uses both a number less than 10 and a number greater than 10 in a comparison. *The halfback gained 5 yards in the first quarter and 77 in the second quarter.* Any number that begins a sentence should be spelled out.

Percent: The AP style guide recently revised how to write percent, which is a common term for students applying to college. Use the % sign when paired with a numeral, with no space—*I am in the top 5% of my class.* For amounts less than 1%, precede the decimal with a zero—*Inflation rose last month by 0.5%.* If you are using the term casually, write out percent as one word—*I don't know what percent of my paycheck to deposit in the bank.*

Qur'an: Can be written as the Koran or Quran. Use Muslim, rather than Moslem. The preferred spelling for the Prophet is Mohammed. Capitalize Prophet when it stands alone when referring to Mohammed. The leader of a prayer in a Muslim mosque is an imam. Imam is lowercase unless it is used as a title before a person's name.

Religious Catholic school terms: There are a number of Catholic colleges whose founding orders have their own style guides for religious terms, including the largest, the Jesuits. If you are writing essays to apply to a specific Catholic school, you should refer to its style guide. Among the most comprehensive style guides are those issued by Marquette University and Santa Clara University. Some general rules: Catholic is capitalized when it is anything religious—*I go to Catholic school.*; it is not capitalized when it means broad-minded or all-embracing—*I have catholic tastes in music. I like all different styles*. Church is not capitalized unless you are referring to a specific church—*I go to church every Sunday. I go to St. Gregory Church every Sunday.* Mass, referring to the eucharistic liturgy of the Catholic church, is always capitalized. *I go to Mass every Sunday.* (The priest says or celebrates Mass; he does not read, perform, recite, or conduct it.) Christ is always capitalized, as is Jesuit, Dominican, or Franciscan. Cross is never capitalized, unless it refers to the specific Cross Jesus was crucified on (and a cross is a crucifix only if it displays Jesus on it). Titles like bishop, archbishop, cardinal, father, sister, and pope are all lowercase, unless they are followed by a specific person's name; then, they are always capitalized. *A new pope was named last year. Yesterday, Pope John XXIII spoke in the Vatican.*

Times: Although most students don't think about it, writing times is one of the most common usages in their essays and in the emails they write to the schools they apply to. The most accepted way of writing "a.m." and "p.m." is with lowercase letters with periods after them. (Some guides suggest small caps with no periods, but those are less widely accepted.) There should always be a space between the time and the "a.m." or "p.m." that follows. *So the correct way to write it is 3:00 p.m., not 3:00pm or 3:00p.m. 3 p.m. is acceptable, but 3:00 p.m. is more formal.* Noon and midnight (neither of which should be capitalized) are neither a.m. or p.m. Do not refer to 12:00 a.m. as midnight or 12:00 p.m. as noon. Just use midnight and noon. Do not use the redundancy 9:00 a.m. in the morning or 3:00 p.m. in the afternoon. If you are referring to a two-hour period of time, for example, 11:00 a.m. to 1:00 p.m., use *from 11:00 a.m. to 1:00 p.m. instead of from 11:00 a.m.–1:00 p.m. "From" requires "to."*

United States/US: Spell out United States when it is used as a noun. *My parents came to the United States when I was three.* US can be used as an adjective. *I would like to join the US Air Force.*

Chapter Nine

Special Usage Rules II

Clichés—In his classic books on writing, the Pulitzer Prize winning writer William Safire warned "***Last, but not least, avoid clichés like the plague.***" He deliberately used two clichés in one sentence to make his point. Clichés are trite, overused words and phrases that are a hallmark of writing without much thought. In a college essay, a cliché stands out (and never say "like a sore thumb") and alerts the reader this essay is likely to be a lump of clay (which is the German derivation of the word cliché; it later morphed into a nineteenth-century French term for a metal printing plate for books that would eventually wear out—like a cliché).

When you write your essay, no matter how good your message is, a cliché or two will doom your chances to write a great essay. Most of the grammar rules and usages that we suggest are meant to make you a better writer; you will not be penalized by the college reader if you do not use them. Using clichés may be one of the exceptions. A reader is almost certain to be turned off by a string of clichés in a 650-word essay.

The list of clichés is practically endless (and don't say "too numerous to count"). To give you an example, here is a sample from US humorist Frank Sullivan,

> My nods are significant. My offers are standing. . . . My motives are ulterior, my circles are vicious, my retainers are faithful, and my hopefuls are young. My suspicions are sneaking, my glee is fiendish, my stories are likely. I am drunk. Q: Drunk? A: Yes, with power. You know where? Q: Where? A: Behind the throne.

Clichés come in different categories (and never say "all sizes and shapes"). Some were created by great writers, and obviously weren't clichés when they were first used. In the Bible you can find phrases like "the apple of your eye" or "wallow in the mire" (which probably became a cliché the day the Doors' Jim Morrison decided to use it in the rock classic "Light My Fire"). These were wonderful words "once upon a time" (don't use that phrase in your essay) but are regarded as clichés today. Shakespeare coined some brilliant phrases—"short shrift" (*Richard III),* "neither here nor there" (*Othello*), "the be-all and end-all" (*Macbeth*), "wild goose chase" (*Romeo and Juliet*), "heart of gold" (*Henry V*)—but you wouldn't want to use them in your essay. Great writers from Jonathan Swift to George Orwell railed against writing that included these types of clichés. Orwell once wrote, "Never use a metaphor, simile, or other figure of speech which you are used to seeing in print."

Some clichés just evolved over time. Good examples include "clear blue sky," "read between the lines," and "time flies." No one knows where they came from. Clever writers have turned a cliché into a humorous saying—"time flies like an arrow; fruit flies like a banana." Groucho Marx memorably did this with his quote, "outside of a dog, a book is man's best friend; inside of a dog, it's too dark to read." It's the only time using a cliché is acceptable.

Then there are the modern clichés, the ones students occasionally use like "at the end of the day" and "for all intents and purposes." "NOT!" (Don't use that in your essay.) A special "tip of the hat" (don't use that phrase) goes to words and phrases that are currently popular. A quick visit to Google Ngrams, the site that tracks word and phrase usage, shows that these have "taken off like a rocket" (don't use that, either).

Awesome: Whenever you find yourself using this word, look quickly for another. The word has become so overused that it means everything—and nothing. It typifies the vacuity of the cliché.

Impact: It's a ubiquitous noun that has become a verb, that has become an adjective (impactful), that has become an adverb (impactfully), and finally a cliché. Never use *impact* as an adverb or as an adjective (unless you are talking about an "impacted tooth"). Do not use it as a noun or verb unless you are talking about a dramatic collision or effect *("the meteor impacted the earth with tremendous force,"* "*the* *stock market crash had a huge impact on the American economy"*). In other cases, for a verb use *influence* or *affect* in place of *impact*: *"the ruling will affect many citizens"* rather than "*the ruling will impact many citizens.*" "*The news influenced my decision*" rather than *"the news impacted my decision."* For a noun, consider *influence* or *effect*. In both cases, impact is not as effective (not impactful) as *"Her friendship had an important influence on me." "The effect of the ruling is unknown."*

Comfort zone: Comfort zone has become such a cliché that even essay prompts use it. This may legitimize it somewhat, but avoid the term if for no other reason than thousands of writers will use it in their essays. It's lazy writing; find some other way to express your level of comfort. That's the point of avoiding clichés like the plague (don't use that phrase). Their use is symptomatic of lazy writing. Show the reader that you are not a lazy writer. That's the long and short of it (don't use that phrase).

Need to: The phrase "need to" as in *"you need to see this movie"* has become one of the clichés of our time. According to the Google NGram Viewer, use of the phrase "need to" rose 500 percent between 1950 and 2000. Besides becoming a cliché, "need to" has become obnoxious. When you are told, "you need to do something" it implies doing that thing is in some way necessary for your mental, physical, or spiritual well-being. It often carries an unwelcome message and contributes to the general diminution of manners and courtesy in our society.

In place of *need to*, try using *should* or *must*. (Google NGram notes that in the same period that the use of "need to" went up 500 percent, the use of both "should" and "must" went down by 33 percent.) The use of *should* and *must* do not serve as substitute for *need to* in every situation, but in many cases they not only retain the advantage of brevity—one word as opposed to two—but also nuance. *Should* often implies actionable but discretionary advice. When someone says, *"If you want help, you should call me,"* there is an implied volition that is not present in "If you want help, you need to call me." That sounds like more of an unforgiving order.

In most cases, *must* implies taking some action is essential. *"You must do this"* is not much different from "You need to do this"—both of them tell you to take action. But the former implies there may benefit conferred to others rather than simply a personal benefit doing what you are told. Consider the mother who beseeches the fireman going into the burning building, *"You must help my children."* Far different than telling the rescuer, "You need to help my children."

Common Errors

Affect vs. Effect: *Affect* is almost always used as a verb that means "to influence or change." "*The high winds affected the ability of our boat to get to shore.*" It can also be a verb that means to act in a specific way: *"to affect an air of superiority."* Rarely "affect" is used as a noun in psychology when it refers to how someone displays an emotion: *"a flat or depressed affect."* This is essentially the only exception to using "affect" as a verb.

Effect is almost always used as a noun, meaning the consequences or results of an action. "*The effect of the high winds was that our boat ran aground.*" It can also be used as a noun meaning someone's belongings "*personal effects*" or in film terminology "*special effects.*" Rarely, *effect* can be used as a verb in the phrase "*effect change.*" This is basically the only time *effect* would be used as a verb instead of *affect*.

Here's how to remember the difference between the two (besides the specific exceptions). ***Affect* is a verb, an action. *Effect* is a "noun, the end result of an action. *Affect* causes *effect.*** Affect and action both begin with the letter *a*. Effect and end result both begin with the letter *e*.

Apart of vs. A part of: Consider the sentence *"The University of Michigan community in Ann Arbor is something I would like to be apart of."* **Don't ever write this** (even if you're talking about a school other than Michigan). It's wrong on a number of levels. First of all, *apart of* versus *a part of*. You don't want to be *apart of* the University of Michigan (unless, of course, you want to attend Michigan State University in East Lansing). It means the exact opposite of what you want to say. *Apart*, one word, means you want to be physically separated. *A part*, two words, means you want to join the Michigan community. In this usage you can eliminate the word *a* and substitute *part of* for *a part of*. They mean the same thing here.

(We know of one college admissions officer who basically told students in an information session that if their essays contained the phrase, "I want to be *apart* of your college community," their applications would be discarded on the spot. Imagine how many times that admissions officer must have encountered that error.)

Even then, the construction, *"The University of Michigan community in Ann Arbor is something I would like to be part of,"* should be rewritten. *Is something I would like to be part of* is a wordy, passive voice construction. Make it shorter, make it active construction, and make it clearer: I would like to be part of the University of Michigan community in Ann Arbor.

Between you and I vs. Between you and me: Even though many well-educated people write and say "between you and I," the correct usage is "between you and me." The well-known Harvard linguist and psychologist Steven Pinker, who frequently publishes on style and grammar, writes, "between you and I" is "not a heinous error." Maybe not, but it is an error nonetheless. As an article of speech, *between* is a preposition, and "between you and me" is a prepositional phrase. Prepositional phrases take object pronouns. *Me* is an object pronoun, and *I* is a subject pronoun, which is why *me* should be used in the prepositional phrase. (The confusion comes from the fact that *you* is both a subject and an object pronoun. And the error also sounds educated.) You would never say "between we, this looks right." *We* is a subject pronoun, so the correct use is the object pronoun *us*—"between us, this looks right." As this book points out, grammar is dynamic and many usages that were once considered wrong are now considered acceptable. But "between you and I" hasn't graduated yet. It's between you and me.

Classmate, Roommate, or Suitemate: Most authorities consider them all one word, without a hyphen. Class mate, room mate, and suite mate are incorrect.

***Compare to vs. Compare with*:** To compare is to examine the similarities or differences between two things. There is a subtle difference between the two usages. When you are comparing two things and want to point out the similarities, use *compare to. When people ask who the most complete player in basketball is, LeBron James is often compared to Michael Jordan.* When comparing two objects or concepts and want to point out the differences, use *compare with. You can't compare heavy metal with classical music; they are two different art forms.*

Comprise vs. Compose: To *comprise* means "to include" or "to contain," in the sense of the whole includes or contains the parts (you can tell if you are using comprise right if you can substitute "is made up of"). *The United States comprises fifty states.* When you use the word *comprise*, the whole, not the parts, should always begin the sentence (not fifty states comprise the United States). To *compose* means to make up (you can tell if you are using compose right if you can substitute *make up.*) *Fifty states compose the United States.* When using *compose*, the parts come first. However, with the word *compose* you can use the phrase *composed of. The United States is composed of fifty states. Composed of* is an acceptable usage and basically means the same as comprise. *Comprised of* is never right.

Continual vs. Continuous: *Continual* means frequent, but not all the time; there is a break in the action. *I am continually getting spam phone calls from telemarketers. Continuous* means all the time, without stopping. *The water from the river is continuously running down the waterfall.*

Every day vs. Everyday: *Every day* are two words that mean "each day." *I have a cup of coffee every day. Everyday* is one word and it is an adjective that means common or ordinary. *Playing piano takes my mind off my everyday concerns.*

Farther vs. Further: *Farther* refers to distance (think "far"). *I live farther from the school than you do. Further* refers to everything else in term of metaphorical distance. *I don't wish to discuss this any further.*

Fewer vs. Less: Use *fewer* for things you can count. *There are fewer plants in the desert than in the rain forest.* Use *less* for things that are not countable. *There is less sand in the rain forest than in the desert.* There are several exceptions to this general rule: distance, time, money, and weight. *I live less than ten miles from you. It takes me less than twenty minutes to get to your house.* (Note that all your essay prompts use the phrase "250 words or less." In this case, longstanding custom prevails and makes it an exception to the rule.) The rule for things you can count also applies to number vs. amount. If you can count it, use number. *The number of plants in the desert was small.* If you cannot count it, use amount. *The amount of sand in the rain forest is negligible.*

It's vs. Its: *It's* amazing how often students get this wrong on their essays because the rule is quite simple. It's is a contraction of two words: it is. *It's very simple. Its* is a possessive. *A dog cannot change its spots.*

Lead vs. Led: Many students *led* their clubs or their teams in high school. In their essays, they often miswrite this as "lead." Lead, which rhymes with seed, is the present tense of led, and that is why they are confused. (Another reason is that *lead* is a homophone of *led*—when *lead* refers to the metal element, number 82 in the periodic table it is pronounced the same as *led.*) But remember, it's *"I led my chess team to victory in the state tournament."*

Lie vs. Lay: Basically, *lie* means to recline (on a bed, sofa, the ground, etc.). *I had to lie down after work. Lay* means to put an object other than yourself down. *I am going to lay that book on the table.* As grammar author Mignon Fogerty, an excellent reference, points out one good way to remember the difference is that the songs "Lay Down Sally" by Eric Clapton and "Lay Lady Lay" by Bob Dylan both use the wrong word.

Many vs. So many: Students routinely use *so many* when they simply mean *many*. Use *so* along with *many* when you want to emphasize a large number, rather than as a routine modifier—*Many weekends during the summer my parents take me to the cabin* rather than *"So many weekends during the summer my parents take me to the cabin"* (unless you want to emphasize you are unhappy about going).

May vs. Might: The difference between the two words is subtle. Both words indicate the likelihood of something happening. *May* is more likely than *might*. "*If it doesn't rain today, I may go to the ballgame"* indicates a stronger possibility than *"If it doesn't rain today, I might go to the ballgame.*" There are a couple of exceptions: *Might* is the past tense of *may*. Always use *might* if you are talking about the past. "*Yesterday, I told her I might go*" is correct; *"Yesterday, I told her I may go"* is incorrect. *Might* is also used to indicate sarcasm. *"I might clean the garage if you become president"* would indicate you think neither is going to happen. The rule to remember is to use *may* if you think something is likely to occur, and use *might* if you think it is unlikely or when you are using the past tense.

Principal vs. Principle: *Principle* is always a noun and it means a moral belief, a law, or a rule. *"I have principles"* is what you say when you want to emphasize you would not do something against your beliefs. If you want to teach good writing, you would teach *the principles of good writing. Principal* can be a noun or an adjective. When *principal* is used as a noun, it means a person in charge, *"the principal of the school."* When referring to the head of a school, always remember *"the princiPAL is your PAL."* It can also mean the money owed in a transaction before interest is charged. *"My mortgage payment includes the principal and interest."* When *principal* is used as an adjective it means important or primary. *The principal reason I took the job was for the money.* The two words are pronounced the same and are often confused especially in legal matters, where a *principal* is a person or party involved in a dispute, but the dispute may involve a legal *principle* or rule.

Renown vs. Renowned: *Renown* is a noun, which essentially means fame. *Renowned* is an adjective, which essentially means famous. If you are talking about a professor or researcher who is well-known, then the correct term is that "she is a *renowned* professor." Alternatively, she is a professor of some *renown*. But she is not a renown professor.

Should have vs. Should of: *Should have* is right. *Should of* is wrong. *Many students who wrote "should of" should have known better.*

This past vs. Last: Many students who write their essays in the fall talk about what they did "this past summer." *Last* summer is preferable to this past summer.

Say what you mean—other words and phrases to avoid include some of the following.

To have the opportunity: In their supplemental essays students often write something like *"I want to have the opportunity to study abroad."* Occasionally, they are actually talking about the chance to do something rather than actually doing it, but in most cases what they actually mean is *"I want to study abroad."* To have the opportunity is generally just empty chatter. Omit it if possible.

To be able to: Another empty phrase is *to be able to*. When you say *"I would like to be able to attend the University of Wisconsin,"* that isn't what you want to convey. Step right up and say *"I would like to* *attend the University of Wisconsin."* These are three words you can get rid of whenever you see "to be able" to.

Reach out: When communicating with a school official, especially in emails, students commonly use the phrase, "*I am reaching out to express my interest in your program"* or "*I am reaching out to see if I can arrange an interview."* "Reach out" is usually unnecessary and often causes you to use too many words to express what you want to say. What you really want to say is *"I am interested in your program. Can I arrange an interview?"*

The times, they are a'changing—here are some once unbreakable rules that may now be breakable: Certain rules of grammar were once immutable. But usages change over time and what was once unacceptable is now seen even in formal writing. We suggest sticking with the long-established rules, but if you feel more comfortable breaking these rules, only traditionalists may object.

Hopefully: *Hopefully* was once an adverb that meant "with hope." *I looked at the report on my grades hopefully.* Today many, if not most people, use hopefully to mean "I hope" or "it is to be hoped." *Hopefully, we will make it to the airport on time.*

Splitting infinitives: If there is a rule to be broken, this is the one. Most of the time an adverb should be placed after the verb in an infinitive construction *He decided* to look closely *at the item in the window.* But if you want to emphasize the adverb, there is nothing wrong with splitting the infinitive. In fact, the most famous example of a split infinitive is also probably the best example of why you should. It is the famous Star Trek opening, *To boldly go where no man has gone before.* Boldly does not fit anywhere else in the sentence.

Ending a sentence with a preposition: This is a rule that is "more honored in the breach than in the observance." (It's actually *honoured* in the original British because this is a Shakespearean quote from Hamlet. And it is *breach*, a violation or breaking of a rule, not *breech*, the back end of something.) *That's a fancy way of saying "never end a sentence with a preposition" is not really a rule.* The best example of why this should not be a rule is a quote attributed to Winston Churchill, *"That is a rule up with which I shall not put."* (Like so many other quotes attributed to Churchill, it may not be true that he actually said it.) Obviously, this shows how silly it is not to say "*That is a rule I shall not put up with*"—*with* being the preposition. The problem is that many people were taught that it was a rule and still believe that it is. So in deference to the reader who believes in it, avoid doing it if possible—try rewriting the sentence, but don't go out of your way and wind up creating an unreadable one. If Churchill, or whoever said it, really wanted to avoid ending the sentence in a preposition he could have said, "I shall not put up with this rule." But that would not make the point.

Plural everyone/their: Traditionally, everyone (or everybody) was a singular noun. *Everyone was (not were) here.* As such, it required a singular pronoun. *Everyone brought* his *gloves.* When everyone referred to men and women, or the sexes were indeterminate, this created a problem. *Everyone brought* his or her *gloves*, a sentence which is admittedly unwieldly. It was formerly wrong to use the plural pronoun *their* in that situation. However, now *everyone brought* their *gloves* has received a general level of acceptance.

The reason why: *The reason why* used to be considered redundant. *The reason why we took the trip is that we had vacation time* says exactly the same thing as *The reason we took the trip is that we had vacation time* or *We took the trip because we had vacation time.* Many people now consider *the reason why* acceptable. The same is true of *The reason is because,* where *because* is redundant but now accepted. This is a situation where we suggest you stay with the traditional "The reason is." *The reason is* the newer versions use more words but are no clearer.

Unique: *Unique* means "without like or equal." *His car was unique in that it was the only one ever made.* Although unique should not be qualified, many people today write "very unique" or "truly unique," and this has gained some acceptance. In general, use the descriptor *unique* sparingly; outside of snowflakes, there aren't that many things that are unique.

Finally, about spell-check.

Spell-check is vital, but be careful. *When you have finished your essay, you must use spell-check for an initial edit.* It will identify commonly misspelled words. It's helpful when you have hit the wrong key because you were typing fast; for rules like "i before e"; and for words you think you know how to spell but don't. Everyone has those problems, and spell-check can identify them quickly.

But spell-check doesn't know the difference between rain, rein, or reign. (It's *rain* that is part of the weather—*rain waters the grass*; *rein* for something you want to take control of—*the president wants to rein in spending*; and *reign* for something that rules—*the Queen reigns over her subjects*. The correct expression is "*free rein*" not "*free reign.*") Spell-check doesn't know the difference between *their* and *there* or *your* and *you're*. So that means that after you have checked your essay with spell-check, you must read it over and make sure that the bell you were writing about at your school was *pealing*, not *peeling*.

Chapter Ten

Editing

You have finished your final draft, but you are not finished. Now comes the edit. You should choose one or two people to help you edit your essay. Do not choose too many people because too many editors can muddy your voice. Listen to those editors, be they teachers, parents, or trusted others. They're not always right, but they are your best hope to hone your essay—and avoid embarrassing mistakes. But, here's the tricky part; don't let them convince you to write something that makes you feel phony or uncomfortable. Editors are invaluable. You can't do this without them. But trust your instincts too. If something strikes you as insincere or over the top, then it is likely to be. **Remember, the final edit is always yours.**

When you edit your essay, you have three goals and you must meet all three: (1) tell your story clearly, (2) ensure you are not confusing the reader, (3) come in at or under the word count. To accomplish these goals, there are two aspects to editing your paper—content and style. The content edit is to make sure you have put forth your story in an understandable way for the reader. This may involve taking out extraneous details or unnecessary sentences. Occasionally, if space permits, you may want to add sentences for emphasis to clarify your message. The style edit is to guarantee that every word and every sentence is exactly what you want to say as concisely as possible.

Here's a little tip when you begin. The word count of your final draft is important. The more the draft exceeds the word limit, the more content you must remove. If your final draft is at or under the word count, you can do either edit content or style or do them simultaneously. You don't have to worry about meeting the word count because you are already there.

If your essay is less than 10 percent over the allotted word count, do a style edit first. You may not have to remove any content. If your Common App essay is more than 650 but less than 715 words, or your 250-word supplemental essay is 275 words, you may be able to get down to the required word count without changing your essay but merely by rewriting your sentences so they are shorter and tighter. This is where you change "*the reason being that*" to "*because*" (three words saved immediately). "*He did not understand, and he was not often on time*" becomes "*He was confused, and he usually came late.*" In the second sentence you've said the same thing, made it clearer, and saved three words. Those words saved add up as you try and get down to the limit.

When your essay is more than 10 percent over the limit, it's extremely hard to get down to the word limit simply by rewriting your sentences (saving 25 words with style editing alone is easier in a 650-word essay than it is in a 250-word essay). This means you may have to prioritize the points you are making—and take out content you might want to keep in. (Experienced writers have a term for this, believed to be coined by William Faulkner—"killing your darlings.") That means don't get too attached to a favorite sentence, turn of phrase, or metaphor. Often the ones that you most adore are the ones that just . . . don't . . . work. Ironic, but true. Good editors will help you excise or fix belabored passages and phrases. Sometimes you just have to do it. It's extremely difficult to shave 100 words or more off a Common App essay without killing some of your darlings.

As with so many other writing tips, there is no best way to edit your essay. These are our suggestions. First, send it through spell-check for spelling and grammar for obvious errors. Because you may have asked others (remember, not too many) to edit, see what they say before you edit. You should not blindly accept their suggestions, nor should you discard them out of hand. After reading their changes ask yourself two things about each change: Does it improve how I tell my story and does it make my essay sound better? Then decide whether to incorporate that specific change.

Taking suggestions from others requires humility. Don't take criticism personally. The best example of this comes from the movie *All the President's Men*, screenplay by William Goldman, who was one of the best screenwriters of his generation. In one scene, the neophyte reporter, played by Robert Redford (the actors are not important in case you are unfamiliar with them), hands in a story he has just typed. Another, more experienced reporter, played by Dustin Hoffman, who happens to be working on the same story grabs it from the desk and starts editing it. Redford is outraged, but Hoffman calmly explains to him why what Redford wrote was unclear. They argue and finally Hoffman says, "Read it both ways. If you think yours is better, use it." Redford reads them both, puts his version down and says humbly to Hoffman, "Yours is better." After that, they become partners on the story. Goldman's point in that scene is that it takes humility to recognize that someone else might be able to improve your writing.

Once you have considered others' edits, it's up to you. The first thing we recommend is that you read the whole essay aloud (either from a printed copy or from your screen). Quite often your ear will pick up something your eye doesn't see. (This is a good way to pick up a word you wrote twice in a row if spell-check missed it.) Something may not sound right, you see something you think you can leave out, or you may think of a better way to say it. Does your introduction make the reader want to read on? Are there transitions between paragraphs? Is the conclusion strong enough? Finally, does the essay tell the reader about you? If you're satisfied on all those counts, put it down and come back to it in a day or so (this is a good reason you don't want to wait until the last day).

When you come back to your piece, the next step is to read it sentence by sentence. Have you followed general grammar rules? Is each sentence clear and concise? Have you written any ambiguous sentences? (Example: *I saw a girl in a boat on the lake with my binoculars.* Who has your binoculars? Are you using them or does the girl in the boat have them?) Look at the adjectives and verbs you used. Are they right or could you pick better ones? Did you make any spelling mistakes spell-check might have missed? (One of us recently wrote a sentence using the term *vice grip* to indicate entrapment. Spell-check didn't flag it because both words were spelled correctly. A sharp-eyed editor pointed out that the correct term is "*vise grip.*")

One of our favorite editors had a saying, "If someone put a gun to my head and said, 'Remove one sentence from each paragraph (because that will pick up the pace),' what sentences would I remove in order to save my life? Then remove 'em." Good advice.

When you are done with your line-by-line corrections, read the whole essay one more time. This is your final read. Does it sound right? If you are satisfied, you're done. Move on to your other essays or whatever else you have to do to finish your application.

Some students don't like to change their essays once they have written them, but good editing is almost as important as good writing. Remember every writer benefits from a good editor.

Chapter Eleven

An Interview with an Experienced College Counselor

As part of this book, one of us sat down to discuss college essays with Jim Conroy, a retired college counselor with forty years of experience at New Trier High School in Winnetka, Illinois. During his time at New Trier, one of the country's top high schools, Conroy was frequently quoted in national publications including the *New York Times*, the *Wall Street Journal*, and the *Atlantic.* As the chairman of post-high school counseling at New Trier, he met with thousands of students and read just as many essays. The following are his shared thoughts:

What is the intent of the Common App essay?

The Common App essay has three purposes. First, colleges want to see if you can put together coherent sentences in the King's English. Second, they want to see if you can follow directions. I have had students tell me they know what they are supposed to do, but they decided they would go a different way. I have to tell them, "no, no, no, this isn't a multiple choice. There is no B, C, or D. There is only A." Finally, the colleges want to see if you can answer the prompt. You have to answer the prompt. And you must remain under the word count.

What are some of the most important do's and don'ts?

The most important thing is "do no harm." Don't dig a hole for your application. Don't be negative. Be positive. Your application tells the schools about you, but in your Common App essay you should tell the school what they don't know about you: your values, what excites you, something you could write 2,000 words about, if they gave you that many words.

You want to revise your essay after you've written it, but don't beat it to death. And don't spend too much time on it. I've had students whose grades went down because they concentrated too much on their essay and not enough on their grades. That doesn't make sense.

How should the student appeal to the reader in the essay?

Of course, you want to gear this for the reader, but that is not as easy as it sounds. Remember, you're not writing for one reader, you're writing for many readers (assuming you apply to several schools). And they may be very different. What appeals to one, may not appeal to another. I can think something is great, but the reader might not think so. But certain things are important. Be honest. Never make anything up. Something is either true or it's not. There are things called honesty and integrity.

What are things that will turn off the reader?

There are obvious things, and there are more subtle things. Use words you use every day. Don't use words or phrases that are not part of the vocabulary of a 17-year-old. I once had a student writing about his experience as a camp counselor. In his essay, he kept referring to the kids as "youngsters." That raised a flag to me; you wouldn't use that word in that setting. When I asked him about it, he admitted his writing teacher had written that. Readers can tell that kind of thing very quickly.

Then there's plagiarism. Do not take off on what's already been done. There are books that present 100 successful college essays—don't think you can take one of those or even borrow closely. You can't. (When I mentioned to him that our book included typical college essays, he said that was acceptable for kids to look at style or get ideas about what to write—but not to copy.)

Are there things that students should avoid writing about?

There aren't many, but there are some things you should stay away from, especially things where you may be portraying yourself in a bad light. Stay away from certain things. I had a student who wanted to write about how she changed her life after she was caught drinking at a football game. I told her not to go there. She said, "But it's about how I changed my life." I said she should think about writing about something else. Politics is not off limits, as long as you frame your essay in the context of a mature dialogue.

Are there things that students should write about?

Not really, pretty much everything is open. I've read about things you wouldn't expect, but they were great essays because they were delightful, genuine, and real. One of my favorites was about a girl who got a lot of stuff done sitting in the middle of the bathroom. She had a large family, lots of brothers and sisters, so that's where she went to concentrate. But she talked about her family, and it was wonderful. So many kids are under pressure because they haven't discovered the cure for cancer. But we have to help them get beyond that.

What role should parents and friends play?

Parents and friends can help kids brainstorm. It's actually an opportunity for kids and their parents to have a good dialogue. Some kids don't have a great memory for things like when they stood up for something. This is where parents can help them. But it's not the parents' role to write the essay or micromanage it. Sometimes it's better to let the kids step in and say "this is what I want to say." Ultimately, it is their essay. We are there to help them.

How important is the Common App essay?

In terms of priorities—grades, test scores, activities, recommendations—it's in the middle of the pack. I can't think of a college that ever called me and said "what a great essay." And in fact, with the increase in applications in the past couple of years, some are just not going to be read. If you have a 26 on your ACT, Harvard is not going to read your Common App essay. But your Common App essay may go to many schools that will read it, and you should give yourself every opportunity to make a good impression.

What is one thing your experience has taught you that most people might not know?

Admissions people respect kids' opinions. Give them space.

Chapter Twelve

You Hit the Submit Button. Now What?

Essays and other work finally completed, you take a deep breath and hit the application "submit" to your first-choice school. *Please heed: Don't wait until five minutes before the midnight deadline to dispatch your application.* There are too many things that can go wrong and cause you to miss the deadline. Your computer can freeze, you could discover that you are over a word count and the essay box on your application automatically rejects it, you may fail to notice an error that is hard to correct, or you encounter some personal issue at home. On the college end, hundreds or even thousands of students may wait until the last minute to file—crashing the school's servers. It may not be your fault that you get locked out, but at the least you may find yourself emailing the admissions officer sheepishly explaining why your application is late. And with a crush of applications, schools might be looking for any reason to reject yours. It may not be fair, but it happens. That's why you should plan on filing at least twenty-four hours before the deadline.

What to Do if You Are Rejected by Your First Choice

When you receive a rejection notice from your school of choice, an initial period of disappointment or shock is understandable (try to stay away from social media, it probably won't help your disappointment). Grieve for a brief period, but realize: *It's not personal.* The odds are you will never find out why you were rejected, and it may have nothing to do with your essay or your application. Your application may be good—in some cases, too good. Schools are concerned with their yield, that is, the percentage of students accepted who actually attend. If a college believes you are more likely to attend another school, it may reject you to preserve its yield. In other cases, schools openly admit there are many rejected students with applications every bit as good as those accepted. It simply becomes a numbers game. It doesn't say anything about you.

The screenwriter who we mentioned before, William Goldman *(The Princess Bride* and not coincidentally *All the President's Men*), wrote in direct, simple sentences. He once explained the film industry in three words, "*Nobody knows anything.*" He meant that no one can predict which movies will be successful or why. College admissions are the same; no one really knows anything. A student with a great application who looks like a "lock" can be deferred or even rejected, and another student with a less impressive application might be accepted. What happens in a college admissions meeting room is closely guarded and rarely travels outside the room. Although patterns and probabilities can be identified, no prediction for an individual student is certain until the moment he or she is notified (and even then, students can do things that prompt schools to rescind an admission, a topic we will discuss).

That's why you must have a backup plan in place. If you planned well, you should have applied to other schools besides your first choice. Most people do apply to more than one school, but not everyone does.

Whether or not you have, it's time to reevaluate your situation. Talk to your parents and to your college counselor. You may have to apply to other schools, and you should start your research right away (more applications probably mean more essays to write). Besides applying to other colleges, consider the community college option. Community colleges are an important part of the college process. They can provide a good education, usually at a reasonable price. After time spent at a community college, students can apply to four-year schools, many of which have designated spots for community college graduates. Sometimes, a backup school is a better fit than your first choice. There are plenty of students who attend their first choice and decide to transfer after a year or two. At a backup school, you may get a better financial package, your education path may change, you may meet amazing friends and perhaps even a life partner. Or you may just have a more enjoyable experience.

Finally, if you are still interested in the first-choice school that rejected you after high school, you can reapply after a year or two of college. It means performing well at the school you are attending, and when you apply you will probably have to write to your first-choice school explaining why you want to transfer. Some students eventually do wind up at their first-choice school after going somewhere else for a year or two. Whatever happens, you're better off with a good plan at the outset.

What to Do if You Are Deferred by Your First Choice

If you applied Early Action or Early Decision to your first-choice school, come December you may find out you are in limbo—neither accepted or rejected, but deferred. The school has removed you from the Early Decision pool and placed you along with the applicants in the regular round. This is a good news/bad news situation. The good news is that you have not been rejected. The bad news is most schools ultimately accept only a small number of deferred students, usually in the range of 5 to 10 percent. But there are some things that you can do to enhance your chances.

The schools are still interested in you and your progress; many schools are tracking your visits to their website and how long you stayed at their site (welcome to the twenty-first century). Make sure you check out your school's website regularly while you wait for your decision.

But there are other things they are even more interested in. The first is your grades. The days of coasting academically during your senior year are long past. *You must have good grades in your first semester of your senior year.* Colleges do not like a C in your freshman year, but they may understand it. However, they hate, absolutely hate, Cs on your senior-year transcript. It gives them a reason to put your deferred application in the final rejection pool. It is crucial that you improve every borderline grade. You will have to inform the school of your first semester final grades. If your SAT or ACT score was not great, consider taking the test again. You can never tell when a higher score will make a difference.

Send an email to the admissions liaison expressing interest. Include your first semester grades and updated GPA (both good), any awards or honors you have won, if you have been on a successful team in the fall (e.g., state volleyball championship), and an explanation of why the school is still your first choice. This must be honest and from the heart. Here is a good sample letter from a student (the names have been de-identified) who was initially deferred:

Hello Ms. XXX,

I hope you had a wonderful New Year! I applied Restrictive Early Action to Notre Dame and was deferred. I would like to express my continued desire to attend Notre Dame, and it remains my first choice for college.

Also, I want to update you and let you know that I received the XXX Scholar honor this semester. My current semester grades:

AP Microeconomics: 96%

AP Spanish Language and Culture: 97%

AP English Language and Composition: 93%

Honors Environmental Science: 87%

Honors Pre-Calculus: 88%

Christology: 94%

Graphic Design: 99%

XXX will send my official transcript with my first semester senior year grades soon. I will give my best effort this semester, and I know that I can raise my Bs to As. In early March, I will send you my second semester quarter grades.

Notre Dame is the ideal school for me because its community is rooted in Catholic values, which are extremely important to me. Notre Dame is also the perfect place to explore my many interests with the First Year Advising program and the flexibility of not having to declare a major until the end of sophomore year.

I want to go to an excellent academic institution with a caring environment. On the school tour, my guide said Notre Dame is a top-ranked academic institution, and students are devoted to helping each other succeed in and outside the classroom. I feel I would thrive in this setting and this community. I would be honored to attend Notre Dame.

Thank you for your consideration.

Sincerely,

XXX

Some colleges will take letters of recommendation for your application. You might ask in your email if you can have someone send a letter or an email of support. *Seek out any help you can.* You may have people in your corner who will support you—high school counselor, senior teacher, coach, important alumnus. See if one or two of them—but not all of them—will write a letter in support of you to the admissions committee.

You must show interest, but remember not to become a pest. Don't contact the admissions people too often. Quality, not quantity.

What *Not* to Do if You Are Accepted by Your First Choice

Notice the difference here—what *not* to do. Technically, you are not actually accepted; it is a provisional offer. You are accepted provided that you do nothing during your senior year that would make the school rescind your acceptance. More than one student has been accepted to college and then had to face the embarrassment of having his or her acceptance withdrawn. Sometimes that happens so late in the academic year that the student has no options (in addition to the fact that what caused the revocation may cause other schools to shy away). Don't worry, though, because this is one aspect of the admission process that is totally in your control. Many things may provoke a school to rescind your acceptance. *They fall into three general categories: academic performance, honesty,* and *misbehavior.*

By far, the most common reason schools revoke an admission is because of a student's academic performance. Colleges monitor how you are doing during your senior year and you cannot afford to let your grades slip. Colleges don't buy "senioritis" as an excuse. *This means maintaining your GPA and especially no Ds or Fs.* It's a red flag when someone who has received all As and Bs for three and a half-years suddenly has Cs and a D during their senior year. It goes without saying you should not fail any courses during your senior year of high school.

Schools expect their students to be honest. *This means you cannot lie on your application*; schools are harsh if they discover that you failed to report a past involvement with the law. *You cannot burnish your resume with courses you did not take or things you did not do* (the 2019 college admission scandal had applicants playing for sports teams in sports they never participated in). Dishonesty also encompasses cheating. If you are caught cheating, it will almost certainly be reported to your college, and the school may revoke your admission. *Likewise, falsifying term papers and plagiarism*. You cannot buy a term paper. As for plagiarism, colleges are intensifying their efforts to root it out. Some high schools and colleges use plagiarism tools to detect work that has been taken from other sources. (Don't even think of "borrowing substantially" from any of the essays in this book!)

Finally, misbehavior. This covers a wide range—everything from a senior prank gone wrong during prom or graduation to criminal behavior. Senior pranks may be fun, but high schools and colleges frown on them. Anything that would jeopardize your graduation from high school will probably force a college to rescind your admission, because, well, you have to graduate high school. A felony arrest—drunk driving, sexual assault, drug offense—must be reported to the school right away, even if you are not guilty (especially if you are not guilty). *Also, be aware of social media.* Students have had their admissions revoked because they have been involved in cyberbullying, have posted inappropriate messages on Twitter, or have had inappropriate pictures displayed on Instagram or Facebook. Think before acting.

Chapter Thirteen

What if You Don't Get Your First Choice? A Final Hint: Life Doesn't End

As we have mentioned several times in this book, college admissions are unpredictable and inscrutable. Two students with equally impressive applications often end up on two different paths.

One gets the congratulatory email and letter; the other a clipped condolence.

One thing every student should know: A rejection from your school of choice is not a tragedy, or a portent of an unhappy life. Tens of thousands of outstanding students are snubbed every year. That's because admissions committees must make difficult choices based on a variety of criteria. They are forced to choose one student with high scores and a long list of extracurriculars over another with equally compelling grades and activities.

So, don't dwell on rejection. It stings, but it fades. It says nothing about your merits, your character, or your future. Those things are determined by you, no matter what college you attend.

Getting rebuffed from a famous Ivy League school can ignite a student's passion to excel, proving in time that college admissions officers aren't infallible or even all that insightful about who has the right stuff to succeed in college, and in life.

As one of the coauthors of this book wrote several years ago in the *Chicago Tribune*, "An admissions committee can't peer into the soul of the child and predict who will do great things with limited abilities, or who will squander natural gifts."

Just as there are many excellent students vying for limited spots across the country, so too are there many outstanding universities competing for students. The difference between a first, second, and third choice may turn out to be negligible. That's because every college has a cadre of inspirational teachers and a vast palette of social possibilities.

If you got into your first school, congratulations. If you didn't, time to regroup. Wherever you go, a great education beckons.

Resources

This book is intended to help you write your college admission essays, but it also has a larger purpose: to help you write in general. Breathe a sigh of relief when you finish your college essays, but you should realize your writing journey is only beginning. You will be writing for the rest of your life—everything from e-mails to term papers, dissertations, graduate school and job applications, recommendation letters, or maybe even your own book someday (*someday* refers to an indefinite time in the future, *some day* refers to one definite day in the future that may be unknown or unspecified).

We are honored that you chose this book to begin your journey, and we wish to recommend other books that will help you along the way. Please don't roll your eyes, we know books are out of fashion, and in consideration of that, we have recommended some useful websites in our text. But we believe, if you plan on writing and doing it well, there are certain books that you might want to have on your shelf. It is certainly not an all-inclusive list, and bear in mind that there is no such thing as the definitive resource. In fact, you are likely to find some disagreement between different references on style and rules of grammar. Don't worry; just use the following books, others that you might come across, some good websites, and (we hope) this book to learn about good writing and create your own personal style.

The essentials, the best basic books on writing in general:
The Elements of Style by William Strunk Jr. and E. B. White
On Writing Well: The Classic Guide to Writing Nonfiction, 30th Anniversary Edition by William Zinsser

One of our favorite authors, an expert on writing style:
How Not to Write: The Essential Misrules of Grammar by William Safire

There is no better book for improving your writing:
Dreyer's English: An Utterly Correct Guide to Clarity and Style by Benjamin Dreyer

General resources:
The Chicago Manual of Style
The AP Stylebook, 55th Edition
Merriam-Webster's Collegiate Dictionary
Roget's International Thesaurus, Eighth Edition
Bartlett's Familiar Quotations

In your writing career, you will find other books that you will make your favorites. It is our hope this will be one of them.

Index

About the Authors

Cory M. Franklin was Director of Medical Intensive Care at Cook County (Illinois) Hospital for twenty-five years. Before retiring, he wrote more than eighty medical articles, chapters, abstracts, and correspondences in books and professional journals. He worked as a technical advisor to Harrison Ford and was one of the role models for the physician character Ford played in the 1993 film *The Fugitive*. Dr. Franklin has been a frequent freelance contributor to the *Chicago Tribune* op-ed page and Editorial Board. His work, medical and nonmedical pieces, has been published in the *New York Times*, *New York Post*, *Dallas Morning News*, and *Los Angeles Times* as well as being excerpted in the *New York Review of Books*. His freelance work has also appeared internationally in *The Guardian* and *The Jerusalem Post*. His books include *Cook County ICU: 30 Years Of Unforgettable Patients and Odd Cases, Chicago Flashbulbs, The Doctor Will See You Now,* and *America's State Fair Impresario: The Life and Times of Michael Barnes*.

Suzanne Franklin is a college counselor and the founder and president of Franklin & Associates, a midwestern college consulting firm. Formerly a social worker, she received an advanced degree from the renowned Family Institute at Northwestern University. She has more than fifteen years of experience helping students from the United States and the United Kingdom with admission to their choice of schools (everywhere from local community colleges to the Ivy League and most of the other top one hundred schools on the *US News and World Report* list of best colleges). She has received the Helen Bruns Ryan Award for outstanding service from Josephinum Academy of the Sacred Heart in Chicago, Illinois.

Linda Black became interested in college consulting starting with her own children, and she joined Franklin & Associates in 2016. Linda graduated from Denison University with a degree in economics. Prior to receiving her law degree from Case Western Reserve University, she worked at a consulting firm in Washington, DC. After graduating from law school, she practiced corporate and real estate law for ten years at Calfee, Halter & Griswold LLP in Cleveland before relocating to Chicago, Illinois.

Paul Weingarten was the *Chicago Tribune*'s Associate Managing Editor for Metropolitan News, a prize-winning writer, and most recently served on the newspaper's editorial board. He and his metropolitan staff won two Pulitzer Prizes during his tenure. In a stint on the *Chicago Tribune Magazine*, he earned several writing awards from local and national organizations. As a national correspondent based in Dallas, he traveled through a wide swath of Texas and the Southwest. On the editorial board, he specialized in a variety of subjects, including education, national security, the Middle East, and health care. He now works as a media consultant and volunteers with journalism students at New Trier High School in Winnetka, Illinois.